ONCE SAVED ALWAYS SAVED

SATAN'S GREATEST TRICK

STEPHEN PIPPIN

WESTBOW
PRESS®
A DIVISION OF THOMAS NELSON
& ZONDERVAN

This book is a work of non-fiction. Unless otherwise noted, the author
and the publisher make no explicit guarantees as to the accuracy of
the information contained in this book and in some cases, names of
people and places have been altered to protect their privacy.

Scripture taken from the King James Version of the Bible.

WestBow Press books may be ordered through booksellers or by contacting:

WestBow Press
A Division of Thomas Nelson & Zondervan
1663 Liberty Drive
Bloomington, IN 47403
www.westbowpress.com
1 (866) 928-1240

ISBN: 978-1-5127-0435-8 (sc)
ISBN: 978-1-5127-0437-2 (hc)
ISBN: 978-1-5127-0436-5 (e)

Library of Congress Control Number: 2015911838

Print information available on the last page.

WestBow Press rev. date: 8/6/2015

TABLE OF CONTENTS

INTRODUCTION

I am well aware of the sensitivity of this subject. I am not in any manner attempting to stir up a bee's nest with this work. I am only aiming to deliver someone from the grip of ignorance in which can cost them the most precious gift from God - their soul.

If you already are aware of my former beliefs and background, let me save you some time by advising you to skip the first six chapters of this book and begin directly in chapter seven. If you would like to know what I did under the belief of *once saved, always saved*, begin reading from the first.

I would ask of you to have an open mind, heart, and much patience with me in my explanations of this very crucial and all-important issue. If you are not a Christian, perhaps this will bring you into the fold of our glorious flock. But this writing is primarily for the Christians in which love Jesus Christ with everything. It is for those in whom are confused about sound doctrine. It is for both young and old alike. If you are reading this, it is probably for *you*.

Many will scoff at me and find this book to be something of a misguided work in which the writer is ill-informed and too amateur and unseasoned in the field of theology to touch on such an important subject. But my ultimate goal and message is to have the readers challenge me and search the Scriptures themselves in order to not be spoon fed that which another claims to be the truth and to find it out for themselves. Don't believe me, but at the same time, don't believe another man as well. Let God be true and every man a liar. This book is dedicated to the Inspiration behind it - the LORD God.

CHAPTER 1

A BIT SURPRISED

Blessed Father, and God of my salvation, how might I explain this truth that Thou may be pleased? Please, O Lord, grant unto me the knowledge with which Thy Name shall be exalted, and show me blameless this day as to my intentions, and that there is no hidden agenda in my heart towards the masses - only love. May the gracious Lamb love me, and show unto them who read this book whatever Thou would have them know, in due time. Blessed be His glorious name, above heaven and earth - forever and ever. A great amen!

I must admit, I'm a bit surprised by the way things have turned out. I grew up believing something that radically changed my perspective on all aspects of life. My belief in one doctrine which I have heard from my youth, from the most influential pastors and my entire household, had grown to be the foundation of life as I knew it.

I would read the Scriptures and find myself subconsciously overlooking certain verses due to the apparent contrast to what I had heard beforehand and believed to be the truth. In essence, I placed that which man told me over that which God was telling me. I have reached a point in my studies, after exhausting myself time and time again, where I can no longer overlook that which I believe to be the truth. Far greater it is to please the Lord God of Abraham, Isaac, and Jacob, than my parents, friends and loved ones.

Several individuals have told me that I should write a book on certain subjects that I have preached on. To every remark, I would reject the notion without giving it even a second thought. But this is too important. I cannot simply preach this to a roomful of people every once in a while knowing that every individual ignorant of this truth could possibly be facing the Almighty God's eternal and infinite wrath! Therefore, having said that, let us proceed.

Each time I would hear of the great warning written in 2 Timothy 4:3, "For the time will come when they will not endure sound doctrine; but after their own lusts shall they heap to themselves teachers, having itching ears; And they shall turn away their ears from the truth, and shall be turned unto fables." I never could have imagined that this may pertain to my own people, my close circle, those whom I love and trusted to give me nothing but truth no matter how difficult it may be to take.

I now see that the fault (if you wish to call it that) is not theirs, but, like me, they had been told of the same doctrine over generations and were simply trusting in those whom they loved to give them nothing but the truth, as I did. I am quite amazed at how much greater Scripture is when one studies it for themselves, rather than remaining dependent upon man to deliver such a crucial Word to their souls.

I suppose I should probably give a bit of my testimony, though I would rather bypass such a thing if it were not relating to the subject at hand. But, never the less, here goes...

I grew up as any typical southern boy finds himself doing: fishing, frolicking, having crushes, being too shy to act on them, you know, the usual. My parents were loving, as were my sisters. There were speed bumps along the way, but love was always the commonality that seemed to hold us together. My parents were young, but were good parents. I see many of my friends and have learned enough of their backgrounds to know that I was fortunate and the Lord blessed us. Though we were by no means rich, or even well off, we, the children, never knew of our parent's struggles. They were always good enough to shield us from such hardships.

My mother always seemed to strive in teaching us the ways of the Lord. The knowledge of the Holy Bible, as well as my own eagerness to learn of God, I suppose, came from the teachings of my mother. My dad always worked and did spend much time with us. He loved us, and we loved him, and that love shall remain all the days with which we are able to love.

As a child I remember hearing of the goodness of the Lord from my mother. My father was not a very religious man, in the beginning, that is. I suppose he was around thirty years of age or so that he came to know the Lord. This was due in no small part to the prayers and encouragement from my mother. Praise the Lord for Godly women! The ungodly women can bring down kingdoms, but a Godly woman can change the world.

So most of my knowledge of the Scriptures came from my mother, and later on, my father. He grew in knowledge rather quickly as I remember. We would sporadically attend church growing up, but regularly attended once my dad was reborn. I can even recall an incident in which another family member made a somewhat snarky comment about my father carrying his Bible everywhere he went by calling him "Bible boy." This never affected him. He had a fire and an obvious passion and desire for God, which, until that time, was quite foreign to the Pippin family.

Piety was a frowned upon thing. For the most part, my father's side was one of rebellion, though there were a few in which obviously loved the Lord. Quite a contrast to my mother's side, which was comprised of very sober and devout individuals. Discipline is what made up my mom's side, an admirable bunch. But the Pippin family was known for their loyalty to one another. If one were down, another would do whatever was within their means to help them get back up. Both families had their good and bad sides (like the majority of families), and equally, I love them both.

I can remember when our local Pastor was preaching one night and how I went forward during the altar call. I felt, as I can only vaguely recall, that it was my time to come forward. After all, I had heard of the Lord, and had a great desire to follow Him, I loved Him, I prayed, I did everything I had heard and felt that a true follower with a yearning to be His would and should do.

I trusted my parents and the preacher. I knew to trust God, so I did. Feel convicted, say the prayer, really mean it, go to heaven, live forever - these were the things that I had been taught and I believed it without flinching. So, I went forward and prayed with the preacher.

I was baptized only a few days later and that I remember fairly well. I also remember constantly praying and having deep faith and never doubting the Lord on anything. I also was quick to defend Him and all of His infallible ways. If you were to ask me now, I would say that I was in God's good grace without a doubt.

Everybody, including the entire church family, were assuring me and congratulating my new acceptance into the kingdom of heaven with the Holiest of holies, King of kings and Lord of lords. I was told that no matter what I did from then on, God would never forsake me and I would be with Him after this life. "What an easy thing," I thought, "why doesn't everybody do this?"

I soon after entered into high school. My influences had gone from parents, to Jesus, but slowly began to go to friends, celebrities, and athletes. I was inebriated by the celebrities of the sports world. I would even say that I idolized them.

I was born March 21, 1984, this was now August of 1998. My circle of friends began to change. My mom was the manager of the cafeteria in my former school of Dodson Branch; so being rebellious was not exactly an option for me while under her watch. When entering high school, however, a sense of liberation seemed to cloud my better judgment.

I was always a fan of hip-hop music. I can recall listening to the more mainstream hip-hop artists of the early 90's. It was around my teenage years that I became obsessed with "gangster" rap.

There was my god - music. Though I had said the sinner's prayer with true faith in Jesus Christ and believed wholeheartedly that I was saved, I began to fall away from the faith. Instead of sweet prayers to God, curse words began to consume my vocabulary. Perverse images were becoming a habitual obsession. Lyrics of sex, drug use and perpetual violence were the only things I would allow to enter my ears. I began to isolate myself from all that was good and wholesome.

Even during this time, though, I can recall sitting and listening to preachers on television, as well as other popular preachers at that time. If there was a Bible story on I would sit and have a genuine interest in watching it and learning. Looking back, I can see a bit of a battle between that which was Godly and that which was evil. Though the evil was a constant, both, due to my seeking it, and due to me being involuntarily exposed to it by my friends, the good would still be presented to me through a movie or in a discussion between my parents on Biblical matters.

Also worth noting is my obsession, at that time, with my own physique. I am a man of short stature - only 5' 5" or so - but my self-esteem was never lacking. My confidence was far greater than any other man that comes to mind throughout my high school experience. I was well aware of my height, this was what urged me to be stronger than the other boys. Not only stronger, but "cooler." I felt a constant need to prove myself. Whether it was through bench-pressing more than others or doing more drugs or fighting, whatever. My want for being exalted above my enemies and friends alike was unmatched.

A good friend (even to this very day) approached me my sophomore year. He wished to start up a music group and inquired as to whether I would be interested in being the hip-hop artist of the group. I agreed. This was to be my outlet for what would turn into years of worshipping my god - music - all the while being told and telling myself that I was saved because of a prayer said years before.

All of my dreams were of self-exaltation (which is unbecoming of a true Christian as we are not of this world and should therefore not desire the esteem of this world). I first loved basketball. I then wished to become a famous football player. After my musical aspiration began, I quit football. This was typical of me at that time. If my interest in whatever I was pursuing or endeavoring to accomplish was found lacking, I ceased in my pursuit the very moment the next opportunity reared its head. This pertained to sports, music, hobbies, girls, friends, whatever was viewed as expendable to me was, most of the time, expended.

My lyrics were comprised of the only things in which my mind was clouded by: sex, alcohol, drugs, suicide, homicide, all the filth of modern mainstream music was what I would speak of. I would on occasion write a song dedicated to God. I rarely spoke of Jesus. Which is strange to say now, because of the obvious reason: He whom proclaims to be a Christian must obviously follow and know Christ! But I scarcely spoke His name. That rarely sold records. My popularity would drop a bit at every mention of the Lord. Even in the "Christian" songs, I could be heard using foul language from time to time. What foolishness!

I graduated from high school in the spring of 2002. After a couple of years and a couple of jobs, I ran into a fellow that introduced me to drugs and promised a constant flow of them if I so wished. I wished. So began my deep, downward spiral into what the word of God says is the "exceeding sinful" and overbearingly obvious life of degradation.

Life seemed to me so simple while under the influence of the Devil's spirits. I remember the first time I had experimented with drugs. I was nine years old. I was ignorant as to what it would do, and what it ultimately was.

From the moment I began seeking God, I was unaware that there were dark forces seeking me.

Forces that were far more advanced and older than myself. Forces that thrive off of human energy and encourage all things wicked to an extent unequalled by man's common desires. I call them demons because that's what Christ Jesus called them. I see it as evidence to the fact that the true title of them is now taboo and medieval sounding to this pitiful "post-modern" wreck of society we currently live in. The more of man we have, the less of God we want. Every technological advancement is simply another toy to put in a person's hand instead of a Bible. Wretched!

But back to the story, this fellow began to sell me drugs. I was at this time around twenty-one. I became quite aware that I had an "addictive personality." The term is almost overused for my taste, as I believe every sinner is susceptible to becoming addicted to sin; It's simply in our nature. But, the same young man, who was about my age, had heard one of my albums. He commented on a "Christian" song I had on there, so he was aware that I claimed the Christian title - he did as well.

We were the most hedonistic of all individuals yet we were both told that if we were *once* saved, then we were *always* saved. You see, he had supposedly been reborn years before like myself, therefore, we were living the greatest life ever - we could do anything we wanted, we never darkened the doors of a church, we never spoke of the Lord, and though we were aware we would eventually die, we were still going to heaven to live forever in even greater euphoria!

What a terrific existence! Oh sure, Christ Himself lived very poor and was overwhelmed with sorrow down here, but that was for Him, not us. I rested on that which I once had - true faith - this is what gave me comfort even when I found myself completely void of that same faith.

CHAPTER 2

THE DARKER YEARS

Father, please give unto your humble servant the ability to remember those things with which I can now say to the reader - to bless them. I wish no deception to partake in this book, my Lord and my eternal Redeemer; my only request is that Thou be with me, a worm, in every memory and all knowledge. May it glorify Thy Name, forever! A glorious amen

My drug use persisted and I, like I said, became addicted to many things along the way. I can hardly remember a single tattoo that I have now that was not inspired under the influence of some sort of intoxicant. I would get high, then begin to write these filthy lyrics (mind you, I still believed fully that I was a Christian), then a new idea for another tattoo would come to mind. Here's the amazing thing about my tattoos which I only recently realized: I have over thirty on my upper body; the vast majority are ironically religious in nature; but what shocks me about them is how they are incredibly self-centered and dark in their meanings.

For example, I have "Shinin'" tattooed on my right forearm. I remember that was the key word I used while writing my lyrics - "shining." Well, the original Hebrew word for the name Lucifer is *heylel* (haw-lale') which comes from the word *halal* (haw-lal') which means, "to be clear; to shine; hence, to make a show, to boast..." No other definition would have suited me more perfectly at that time in my life than the definition of Lucifer, yet I still fully believed that I was following Christ... what nonsensical thinking on my behalf. And my ignorance of this persisted because I was told I was "once saved," therefore, "always saved."

The reason for me writing this book is not to argue. My intention is not to sell books or make people think I may be on to something others have not discovered. My only agenda is to spread the truth by any means that I possibly can. We are dealing with eternity here! This is not a game, therefore, I cannot stand back and allow Hosea 4:6 to play out before my eyes: *"My people are destroyed for lack of knowledge: because thou hast rejected knowledge, I will also reject thee..."*

By this point, you may feel that you already have this book figured out: That I'll tell you that you can lose your salvation and that your works get you into heaven, and this and that. Let me assure you, dearly beloved, if that is what you believe this book will tell you, you are mistaken terribly. Just bide with me.

My life of sin increased to the point of despotism. I never truly knew what it meant to be a "slave to sin," but, in retrospect, I can see it clearly now. I would risk my job, my freedom, my health and, on many occasions, my life to acquire my worldly desire. Be it drugs, alcohol, women, fame, fortune, whatever the object of my affection may have been, I was more than ready to do anything and everything for it.

I was always up to talking to the dope dealer, but I despised cops and preachers; you see, one was a watcher over my physical self; the other was a watcher over my spiritual self. Neither was within my circle of friends and were often mocked and ridiculed whenever they were mentioned among us.

You can often tell an individual by the company they keep. All of my friends were either agnostic or claimed to be Christian. The commonality was that we all used drugs, partied hard, drank habitually, were lustfully driven, and never spoke on spiritual matters. Sure we spoke of death, but almost as a type of scary story. We never allowed it to fully sink in. One could liken our perception of death to that of children daring each other to go into the dark room no one else dared venture into. We thought of it as something far beyond the horizon. A hundred years away, even an eternity away. Something that we heard would happen, but never truly would come to pass. We were blinded by the things before us and gave no thought to those things we perceived to be far away.

One conversation comes to mind in which I discussed with a close friend, during those darker years, the subject of heaven. He told me what most people usually say: "I'm a good guy. I've never killed anybody. I've stop stealing. I try to do my best every day. I mean, I'm not perfect, but neither is anybody else. Yeah, I think I'll wind up in heaven."

Many Christians whom rely upon the popularized version of O.S.A.S. are known for scolding such individuals whom have this way of thinking on being accepted into heaven. They usually liken the individuals who declare that because they are "good" people and focus primarily on their own merit to enter into heaven to those whom do not believe in Eternal Security.

My hope, and prayer, is to possibly clear up such confusion amongst my brethren. Of course our own merit counts for nothing. But there are many things overlooked by those whom skip over certain details of the gospel in order to suit their own beliefs. We should not make the grievous error of forcing God's Word in order so that it conforms to our own. We ought always to strive for the truth, no matter how painful a venture it must be. For this life is a vapor and all of our struggling will not go unrewarded and be for naught.

My then friends and I had many discussions about the afterlife. Never will I forget all of the times people have so boldly proclaimed to me "I don't fear God." They would say this in such a way as to show their reliance on God's love, paying no heed to His just and wrathful nature. Even then, I could not help but feel compelled to adamantly mention my fear of the Lord. I said this in such a manner as to hopefully force a retraction of the dangerous statement they just made. No such retraction was ever made.

I believe this is much the problem with society today. The Book of Proverbs is very clear in stating the necessity of the fear of the Lord in relation to wisdom. Because we have chosen to not fear God, we will be punished. We are heaping up for ourselves more wraths than we can possibly fathom.

Why do I mention this in a book dealing with Eternal Security? It's simple really: This incredibly popular and widely believed doctrine has spread throughout the world. Once again, I would like to stress that this is not a book that runs in stark contrast to the doctrine, only in the popularized teaching of it. Surprisingly, many fundamentalists preach this doctrine throughout the world. Even scholars and famous theologians fully and wholeheartedly believe the popularized version of Eternal Security.

My point in mentioning the importance of the fear of God in relation to O.S.A.S. is this: When an individual believes that after they say the sinner's prayer that all of their past, present, and future sins are forgiven and heaven awaits them after this life, a certain relaxation comes upon them. One preacher was even so bold as to say, "Once you say the sinner's prayer, God will never forsake you. You may forsake Him, but He will never forsake you." That is entirely unbiblical and much blood shall be on the hands of such preachers whom proclaim such an erroneous belief to their people.

Around six months ago, I can recall working on a sermon. The Holy Spirit is Who inspires nearly every word in which I write down, so that particular night the Spirit was upon me and inspired me to ponder on Satan's greatest trick in the world. I actually entitled the message *Satan's Greatest Trick*. This demonic trick in which I was fixated on was that of him telling people that they were saved when, in all actuality, they were just as lost as they ever were. My focus was on the new birth - being reborn. The entire message centered on that of true regeneration; becoming who the world would label as a "Jesus freak;" in other words, becoming all about Christ Jesus.

The point of the message was forcing individuals to self-examine themselves. Who was their true focus? Who was their true God? If they were not all about Jesus, then one could safely conclude that they had been deceived, either by themselves, or by a demonic influence into believing that they were saved when in reality they were not.

I can look back now and see that the Holy Spirit was not wrong in the inspired message which the Comforter gave unto me. But because I was still lacking in my own knowledge of this crucial doctrine, the message was not quite finalized. Only half of the trick was revealed. The intention of this book is to totally expose Satan's greatest trick.

I find it a strange thing that I almost cringed when my friends related me to anything Christian. When playing my album for them I would always begin with the most mesmerizing, and oftentimes, vulgar tracks, then intentionally avoid the only "Christian" song on the record. I believe even at that time such behavior seemed odd to me; my awkward attitude towards anything pertaining to Christ.

On one occasion I remember hanging out with some other buddies (once again, not a one Christian) and being approached by a young Christian boy. There was no way he was older than seventeen or so.

That courageous youngster walked right in the midst of us wolves and simply asked the question: "Does anybody here love Jesus?" Out of the ten or so of us I was the only one to raise my hand and proudly admit, "Yeah, I love Jesus." The boy then proceeded in asking me, "Well, what are you doing out here?" A rush of anger began to consume me, I replied, "Hanging out with my boys." If I can remember correctly, I believe he inquired as to whether or not I attended any church. I told him, "No, a man doesn't have to go to church in order to get to heaven." He replied, "True, but a Christian will naturally want to go to church."

I look back now with admiration at the young man's persistence, none-the-less, I replied, "You're starting to [tick] me off" (language is altered for obvious reasons). He then gently replied back, "Why are you cursing at me if you're a Christian?" Oh, this young man, to have a fraction of his courage and patience. Some other boys began to grab his tracts and, while they were cursing him and stomping his pamphlets on the asphalt, what he said began to stir within me.

Do not mistake me, I was older, meaner, more aggressive, more known, and stronger - but I got put on the spot and brought low by this teenage boy. I mean he absolutely shook me off my pedestal. I will ask my heavenly Father one day to allow me to thank that boy for his courage and determination. He was miles up the road spiritually than where I claimed to be. Even today I would love to meet that young man and give him a big ole hug. He momentarily opened up my eyes to the true manner of Christian living. But even after that incident, I still believed that before, during, and after that confrontation had taken place, I remained in God's grace. *Sure, I may need to clean up a bit, but don't we all* was my thought pattern. I would justify my actions by my circumstances, age, environment, friends, family, whatever. I was very clever in placing blame anywhere but on myself.

I believe that was one of the reasons King David was known as a "man after God's own heart." He thought more of God's feelings than his own feelings; of God's will over his own will; of God's plan over his own plans. After he had sinned with Bathsheba, one can read Psalm 51 to find out where David solely placed the blame - upon himself. He does not blame Bathsheba for bathing within his range of sight, he does not blame Uriah for not going to his home when he told him to, he does not blame Nathan for confronting him - he blames himself.

Taking responsibility for one's transgressions is primary in a Christian's life. The same individuals whom often jump to make an excuse or blame others for their sins are usually the same whom tend to overemphasize grace. This is of the utmost importance in understanding and fully grasping the truth in which I am endeavoring to explain throughout this book.

You are probably asking yourself by this point, "Why doesn't this guy just give us the verses he's read, then explain what he believes them to mean, then simply tell us what he believes?" Well, you have to understand that if I did that, I would only be giving to you a cold and very surface-level explanation of something that is very beautiful and deserving of my own individual telling of what I experienced under the belief of what so many cling to for their way of life and philosophy altogether.

This doctrine is not a minor one in relation to the Christian faith, nor is it a major, it is foundational. This is fundamental. If I serve this to you cold and without properly preparing it beforehand, you may simply skim over it without fully grasping the importance of what I am trying to convey to you. I would also urge you not to mistake complexity for something sinister or deviant. In all truth, what I will show you is not complex, but a very straightforward and plain telling of that which true salvation means in Jesus Christ.

CHAPTER 3

EVEN DARKER YEARS

My Father and LORD of my salvation! O glorious King of all kings! Almighty high and lifted up God of everlasting and ancient days! How might I speak to Thee? Father, grant unto me wisdom to follow Thy will and the understanding to walk in Thy light. O exalted and magnificent God, please be with me in my endeavors, and show me while I attempt to show them all truth. Blessed be His name in which heavens and earth obeys! Amen

As time went on, I fell deeper and deeper into depravity. More tattoos, more booze, more drugs, less money, less control, and ultimately, less faith.

It was around the winter of 2007 that I remember lying on my parent's bed watching the History Channel. I had always had a fondness for history, but this eagerness seemed to increase after high school. Around the end of my teen years, I had slowly began to drift away from watching The Simpsons and King of the Hill and, to my surprise, had found an interest in Fox News, CNN, and, eventually, the History Channel. So there I was, eating, drinking, relaxing, just another lazy day as most others when a show comes on pertaining to evolution.

For those of you not aware of this theory, you can research (though I would not recommend this) *Charles Darwin - evolution* and then add the key word "fraud" if you wish to find out the truth of the mess. It is the belief for all whom wish to not believe in God. It is an escape from the Holy Bible and more people, in my opinion, have missed heaven as a result of it being popularized over any other philosophy ever presented to man.

It claims we are all animals; everything is here by chance; and you and I are not special. Of course the obvious implication of such a belief is that there is no afterlife - no heaven, no hell and, therefore, no judgment. In other words, don't worry about meeting God after you die; there's no such thing as sin; we all only live this one time, so there's no need of us being afraid of what comes after this life. Such a theory is so devilish that we cannot even begin to imagine the ramifications it has wrought forth.

I was intrigued by this theory of evolution - I became bamboozled by it. It confounded me. Though I had heard of it in my biology class in high school, I never paid it much thought. The main reason for me not paying heed to such a ridiculous idea, at that time, was due to me having a hint of faith in the Lord - remember, I had prayed that faithful prayer years before, so I was presumably a Christian, though I presented no true evidence (good fruit) in favor of my Christian faith. Therefore, I was ignorantly on shaky ground.

Many have heard my testimony and simply chalked it up to saying that I was not truly saved to begin with. I disagree with that. I had faith and love and a zeal for God that most others of my age and even older had not shown. I believe now that I simply lost my faith and fell from God, as well as His loving grace. This happens quite often and is one of the primary reasons for me writing this book.

I was so easily persuaded by a simple little program on the History Channel. I quickly grew to believe this dumb theory of evolution. I saw nothing wrong with believing we came from monkeys and continuing my belief in Christ and the Father God.

I rationalized mixing these two completely contrary beliefs together like others whom are called theistic evolutionists, by stating: "Well, God made the monkeys, didn't He?" and "Sure, the Big Bang

happened, but God's the One that made it explode."
No other belief is so contrary to God's Word, yet
people attempt to show compatibility between
the two.

I slowly began to lose my faith altogether.
Desperate for answers to life and searching for them
in all the wrong places, I reached out to anyone
offering what I was seeking.

When I was about twenty-six years old, I was
hired at a factory in Livingston, Tennessee. This was
probably the tenth job I had since high school. I had
been by that point a full-blown addict. I cared for
nothing except me. Sure, I was nice to people, but it
was far from genuine. Even my polite attitude was
self-serving. I was getting high before work, during
breaks, during lunch, and on the ride home. If you
have ever been an addict to that extent, you are
probably aware of the importance of going unnoticed
and without drama.

That was my entire plan. Everybody that I knew
could have died suddenly and I would have only been
momentarily moved until I got my next fix. If you
know me now, you may believe that statement to be
an exaggeration - but it sadly is not. I wasn't a robot
or heartless, but my heart was set on what I wanted
and me - not people, not God. Add to the situation
that I believed we had evolved over millions of years

from a primordial soup in a pond and you have the perfect worldly man mentality all in one being.

But, I was still saved, or so I thought. I had faith, prayed the prayer, feared God, and professed His Son to anyone; therefore, no matter what I fell into believing, no matter what I was doing, I was still going to heaven.

My music 'career' was still in full effect. I had released hundreds of songs, had a dozen mix-tapes, a couple of albums, a single featured in a movie, was beginning to perform locally and was saving up money for a promotional campaign. Ironically, I had another album in its beginning stages entitled *The Awakening*. Little did I know that my life's true awakening was yet to come.

Every month I would have another tattoo added. My focus was on the parts of my body that could be seen. Most folks choose to get them where they can cover them up, not me. I was going to be famous, rich; all eyes were going to be on me. I wanted to look just as *cool* as I possibly could to my fans. My true objective was to have others idolize me. I wanted them to look at me in the same way that I looked at other rappers.

I hated to see others succeed. I would often overlook any good quality in a person in an attempt to spot the negatives and quickly point them out in hopes to demean that person in other people's eyes.

I have since become a bit discouraged to learn how such competitive attitudes are found in nearly every area of endeavors.

They say, "Potter envies potter" and "athlete envies athlete." A ball player may not mind it if you are known as the best swimmer in the world, but if your jump shot proves to be better than his, that's when animosity rears its ugly head. There's a silent competition among preachers as well. I never would have believed such a thing if I had not noticed it first-hand. For such pride to reside within the Body of Christ is a pitiful thing.

I have noticed that when a younger preacher knows something pertaining to Scripture in which an older preacher never noticed, the elder, most of the time, will become angry, then jealous at the younger preacher. Such anger has been directed at me a few times.

If your prayers are more in-depth and sound sweeter, if your knowledge of the gospel is sounder, and if your studies are more apparent and foreboding than the older preachers - young soldiers, beware. Wolves (within a church) are not born they are created. Out of the midst of jealousy, hate, envy, lust, any sinful inkling which makes its abode within a man, be he Godly or sinful, will only bring forth demonic intentions unless it is uprooted and cast asunder.

Think not that such intentions will be withheld from the author of this book due to his young age, and be not fooled by such who may claim to be insulted solely by the subject at hand. Jeremiah 17:9 is quite clear, "The heart is deceitful above all things, and desperately wicked: who can know it?"

One of my favorite preachers had admitted to falling into the trap of competitiveness amongst his colleagues. He brushed this aside as something wretched and I have learned much from him describing his experience. A man has not his eyes upon the Lord when he is focused on others. My advice to all people who walk with God is to focus on His will and nothing else.

When we die, who will be there? Who then will we have to compare ourselves with? Stay the course, good soldier, and fight the fight your Lord would have you engaged in for His name's sake. Worry not if someone is jealous because you are mountains higher than him or her spiritually. I pray you pray on.

The closer one is to the Father, the less he will worry about men. I believe that if I had known that fact at the time of my wildest years, I would have realized that I was not one of His children. But think not that I did not ponder on my lifestyle being contrary to other Christians. I had heard how God demands holiness from His people and was well aware that my 'fruits' were not the fruits of Christ. Still, I was not swayed by such knowledge. I was blinded by this thought that I was saved, would always be saved, therefore, I was destined for heaven.

Such blind steps taken in darkness can only come from the evil one. So certain I was within my being. So assured I was by my own people that I was 'saved.' Nothing could have dissuaded me from this belief - except God. I was under a powerful illusion that had ingrained itself within my very bones.

My every thought, no matter how malevolent or cruel in nature, was given a permit of allowance by this belief which I had held from youth - I was eternal secure, no matter what. Even if I lost my faith in God altogether, I was still heaven-bound. But life, as I knew it, was about to get worse.

The Lord's kindness is not like the kindness of man. He does nothing halfway. When the time comes for a decision to be made He will force even the most wretched of us into a corner where the games stop and eternity is faced. This point was about to fall upon me like the greatest star in this vast universe.

CHAPTER 4

THE CULMINATION

*Please, dear Father, my Lord and Savior,
Whom I love more than my own life, lend
unto me the patience, love, and kindness
required to deliver such a note as this to
Thy people, whom are far more precious
than all the rubies and gold in existence.
Blessed be Thy name, O Father, be
exalted, and may I be humbled so that
Thou brightness may shine through all the
more. A mighty amen!*

Know that I am withholding from you, the reader,
many of the things in which are far too cruel to be
spoken of my actions. I would only have you know
a generalized view of my transgressions as any
specificity of my wretchedness may be interpreted
as a boast. Of such things, I would not wish upon
you. There are memories in which I flinch when they

come flooding back to the forefront of my thoughts due to their vileness. I feel myself without equal in deserving the title "chief of sinners" as I have done the foulest things against my Lord and Savior. I speak not in terms of blaspheming His name ignorantly but railing against Him and Him alone on many occasions.

There is one horror movie in which comes immediately to mind about a demonically-possessed girl. I first viewed the movie at around ten years of age. I was so terrified that I remember the night in quite decent detail. I had begged my mother to watch it. She was the first to warn me against it.

We went to the movie store quite often back then. This was before DVDs and whatnot. We had VHS tapes and thought those were the top-of-the-line products - nothing could get better than that, we thought. Anyways, my mother was always bombarded by, "Can I get this one? Can I get this one?" Normally, she would either say maybe, or yes, but with this particular movie it was always a stern "no." She told me that was the scariest movie there ever was - that made me want it ten times more.

One night though, she finally caved. She said, "Fine, but I will have to fast-forward some parts because they're too bad for y'all to watch." I was ecstatic. We went home and they watched their movies first. I fell asleep and woke up right when the little girl began to bang her head up and down on her bed and the entire bed started shaking. My attention was peaked. We wound up watching the rest of the movie with my mother hurriedly racing toward the screen with a pillow on occasion to shield us from the most atrocious parts.

After the viewing, my older sister and mother went to bed. My father was already in the bed, having not even watched the movie at all that night. My younger sister had fallen asleep and watched not the first minute of that horrible movie. I remained in the living room, wide awake, and I can remember having to use the restroom for the better part of two or three hours and being too petrified to do so.

The reason I mention that experience is that I can look at that little girl now and relate many of my actions to being similar to hers. The more hatred I had for my Creator, the more self-harm I would inflict upon myself. The more I hated Him, the more I hated myself. It is my looking back at that movie that I can safely state that I was demon-possessed. "Oh sure," the skeptic sarcastically says, "you were throwing a temper tantrum and you were demonically influenced to do so." I threw temper-tantrums as a child and never thought for a second to hate God. My primary focus, all my strength, mind, and thoughts were directed towards the heavens.

The most infamous Satanist ever encouraged drug use in order to get in touch with spirits. Remember now, I was a heavy drug user. My ignorance was at such a dismal point at that time that I would praise God when I would safely acquire my drugs. I did not do this in any facetious manner; I truly would thank the Lord as if it was what He wanted for me to have. Do you see the depravity of the sinful man? How confusion overtakes him and carries him into a wonderland of his own making?

I remember the drug-free teacher of my youth, whom continues to love the Lord and help children throughout the years, he once told my class something to the effect of, "Drugs are like the fun room an addict always wishes to be in." Once you are forced out of that room, nothing is fun anymore. It's all a deception.

Life was no fun without drugs. Even eating was a chore without a fix. Watching movies and listening to music, playing video games, reading the most in-depth philosophical writings, everything is boring when an addict does not feel the high.

The only thing, and I'm being serious, that was not enjoyable when I *was* high was reading God's word. Not due to any overbearing conviction, but because I found it to be a rather dull and boring read. I believe it is meant to be that way. Only a sober and clean spirit can experience the love that exudes from those pages. Those wonderful pages! How might I count Thy ways, O God of my fathers! A love unmistakable and undeserved by those whom feel the Lord's presence. O glory and truth!

I despise my old ways and have a deeply rooted regret when I speak on them, but for your sake, I will go a bit further. The Bible, when read by my sober eyes, is a life source. A stream of something in that the world could never mimic. But when I was drunk or high, it felt as if nothing could get through the haze. I could absorb everything else with ease. I remember reading "Trial and Death of Socrates" in awe and Sun Tzu's "Art of War" with such a passion, but I could not hardly absorb anything from the Holy Bible. Now I can read those books and feel only a bit of admiration for their thoughts and philosophies, but the Bible is to me now something otherworldly.

I can ponder on a single verse for a week and learn more than all the old Greek deep thinkers could ever hope to mentally conjure up. A sober mind is needed to comprehend scripture. The prophets were very sober men; as were the apostles and disciples. I often believe that such is the problem with the pharmaceutical drugs prescribed now for depression and anxiety. I have had my fair share of anxiety attacks, but I believe the drugs in which the doctors are now vending out like candy is just as spiritually harmful as Bo-Bo down the street selling weed.

Just a quick note on those anxiety pills: It is written (Revelation 18) that in the last days (which we are currently in) there would be sorceries. The Greek word for "sorceries" is *pharmakeia* (far-mak-i'-ah) meaning "medication, i.e. magic (literally or figuratively)' an alternate word is *witchcraft* (refer to Revelation 21:8). Though I know I'm a bit off the main subject, remember that I am still a preacher, and who better to learn from than someone who has already driven down that road. Watch what you take is all I'm saying.

My sister remarked to me once that I was nicer when I was high, and I have heard from countless people, including members of my family that they are much more tolerable to other people when they take their anxiety medication. But know this, though I was nicer, more loving, and happier while under the influence of drugs and/or alcohol, my thoughts were always on the drug itself. I placed all of my faith and trust in that drug, not in God. I used to be so consumed with being happy. I thought that was all life was about - being happy.

For a supposed Christian to seek happiness in anything besides God is ludicrous and entirely unfounded. There will be no weed in heaven; there will be no Jack Daniels in heaven. Why then would an addict or drunk wish to go? Their god isn't there. I find myself rebuked whenever I state so boldly such an obvious fact. The drunkard will say, "I don't worship this bottle, I worship God." But where does all of his money go? In the offering plate? To the poor? No, it goes to that bottle. The old saying, "Put your money where your mouth is" is quite profound in its implication. The thing in which you apply that which you work the hardest for (money) Is the Instrument in which you can gauge where your heart is. Did not Christ say, "For where your treasure is, there will your heart be also."

I say this to you so that you may know your own stance with God. I have spent thousands of dollars on dope and drinks, all the while believing myself to be a Christian and one of His children. A bit of self-examination can go a long way.

My wicked escapades would only worsen when I turned twenty-seven years old. I was then about six months into my new job, everybody loved me, I had a steady flow of my addiction, and a seemingly happy future ahead of me.

Everything seemed to be great. For the first time ever, everything was perfect. I would wake up and go to work, clock out, go home and party. Fun times all around. My whole clique would do whatever we wanted, whenever we wanted, however we wanted.

The only thing we did not do was discuss Jesus. Cops would be mentioned more than the Son of God. Even Allah and aliens would be more spoken of. A completely devilish environment, yet I seen no problem with it. I was saved and on my way to heaven, didn't care if they were, long as I was - PLUS, I was getting to do everything they did and then some.

Many addicts claim they were "the worst of the worst," I want for everybody to know how well aware that I am of that. But, when I say to you that I was the first to get drunk/high, the first to pass out, and the last to leave - I mean it. I was the guy that would snort something before everybody else to see how harsh it was for him or her.

Everyone in my circle knew that I claimed to be a Christian. The sad part about it: I thought I was, too. My ignorance rubbed off on them. I was a stumbling block. My actions were telling them that it was alright to act like the devil and still go to heaven.

My language was so filthy by this point that you would have thought I knew no other vocabulary than curse words. I had more tattoos than all of my friends combined, yet I was the supposed Christian. None of them ever called me out on it, nor did any of my family members. The only person whom ever called me out on it was a boy that didn't even know me on the street one night. I scolded him for it and watched while he was mocked and ridiculed.

I was so fully convinced of my salvation that I would not hear any voice telling me otherwise - not even God Himself. The voices of my church family, the preacher, as well as my parents, would always flood back to the forefront of memories reminding me that I had faithfully said the sinner's prayer and I was saved forever that night.

Life began to take a turn for the worse after arguments began to spur up between me and my inner circle. My own home began to feel very eerie at night. Even roommates were complaining about it. The lights started erratically flickering. One of my friends and I had heard voices which sounded like little children. All sorts of anger was arising out of nowhere over nothing. It got so bad that I remember asking my supervisor if I could work overtime everyday there for a while. I hated going home. I hated seeing friends, family, anybody.

I soon figured that living by myself would work out better, so I isolated myself from everybody and pushed them all away. It broke my heart to do that, but they were better off without me. I was such a wretch that my boss asked me if I was alright. Nobody had ever asked me that. I said, "Yeah." He replied, "You look a little depressed, Bub." I told him I was. He then tried to cheer me up by telling me at least the gray hair wasn't going to show because I always shaved my head.

A few months later I was headed to work. Just two days before, I had purchased a 47" flat screen television. That same day, my boss had warned me that I had no more days to miss. If I did, I would lose my job. I had no money saved up as I had spent it all on drugs, tattoos, partying, and a new flat screen.

So there I was headed to work. I had just lit my joint when I heard *Boom!* - flat tire. I had no minutes on my cell phone. The second I seen the flat, I didn't even try. I simply said, "I'm fired." That was the day that began the deepest depression I have ever experienced. I truly believe in my heart that I'll never have a lower point from here to eternity.

I went home and got the call the next day that I was fired. I immediately sold my flat screen and began applying for other jobs. A week went by, then two, then a month. I wasn't hearing anything back from the job search. Food was running low and drugs were running out. I began to pray again. Amazing how even the worst of us will turn to God when all else fails. The first resort for a saint is the last resort for a sinner.

CHAPTER 5

THE FALL

Blessed God and Lord of my soul. The One in whom I adore! No other do I go to in asking for comfort and peace! Thy wing encompasses me as I speak Your word and blessed art Thou! Let the whole world rejoice at the sound of the Lamb's call for His own!!! Blessed be His glorious name in which I pray, amen!

Growing up a short man, I must admit to the innumerable times in which I heard the saying, "The taller they are, the harder they fall." I never knew that such a phrase would one day apply to myself. Only the wording would be changed slightly to apply more to my ego than my height: *The higher they are, the harder they fall.*

I had become so "puffed up" that, had I remained humbled, this disastrous portion of my story would be brushed over like any other. Those with a humbled heart see no reasoning in getting so upset over money. But it wasn't just money. I suddenly found myself completely alone. The few friends I had voluntarily pushed away had abandoned me. No girls were hollering my way. My music was at a stalemate. The bills were piling up. My stress was on the rise. For the first time in my life, I truly felt alone.

I would sit and cry, pray, then cry a bit more, then wait. I would wait a day or so, then repeat the process. One instance comes to mind when I had just waked up. The sun was shining on my head. I looked outside at the beautiful day and said, "I'm still here." Of course, I figured that I would wake up again, but my words were that of discontentment. I was so deep in my own mire that I could not enjoy even the most glorious and lovely of things around me.

Remember how I told you that I always believed life was about being happy; well I can recall quite clearly what my prayers consisted of. I would ask God to kill me, to just let me die. I would force through the tears these words, "If I can't be happy, I don't want to live." I could not grasp the point in living without happiness. So I wrote a note.

It wasn't a very long letter. Simply one in which I could tell whoever may have read it that this was no one's fault. I was simply not happy and wished to stop living. The prayer that I prayed after I wrote that was the most intense and serious I had ever been with God up until that point. I had spent most of the days leading up to that cursing God, but especially that day. After the letter was completed, I began to yell out in pain and despair. It was at this point that I remember banging my head against the wall and screaming loudly all sorts of blasphemies.

I know not if I was trying to work myself into a frenzy in order to do the deed or not, but I can now see how dangerous of a situation I was in. I ran into the master bedroom and grabbed my father's .22 caliber pistol. I made sure it was loaded, cocked the hammer and wept profusely. It's strange looking back at it now. I cannot recall much of what was going through my mind at the time. I remember hatred for God, deep depression, and a desire to end everything. One solemn thought that I do remember having was that I was still probably going to wind up in heaven after the ordeal was finished. There was also that moment I thought I might not, but I brushed it aside in light of such thoughts inhibiting progression of the act.

I was not afraid of death, but hell terrified me. I grew weak while holding the gun to my head, so I went from my knees to the floor. As I lay on the floor, I kept the gun to my forehead. I had been hunting many times in my life and knew the sensation I had before pulling the trigger. I would attempt to focus my entire mentality on acquiring the target, then pulling the trigger. Acquiring the target was completed now, all that was left - pulling the trigger.

So I tried to force all of my energy into my thumb. How unnatural this whole ordeal felt to me. The coldness of the tip of the barrel on my forehead. My thumb, instead of my finger, on the trigger. This instrument of death pointed at me, by me. Eternity but the blink of an eye away. I eased some energy into my thumb, closed my eyes and braced for death. So many hateful and selfish thoughts were swarming my brain. So many thoughts on who might find my body. What they would do when they found it. How sad and traumatized they would be. *Hopefully the letter would give everyone a little comfort* is how I rationalized it. The most profound thought was that of what, or Whom, I was about to see - or not! In my heart of hearts, I knew that I would go to hell, but my hatred for this life was to such a degree that I didn't really care.

Pull it! Pull it! Pull it! said all of my thoughts in agreement with the spirits. *It will never get better,* and *I'll finally get to rest in peace.* These were what made up the entirety of my psyche at that moment. But then - it all got quiet. In an instant, I heard a clear voice say to me, *Look up* (more was said but certain details are being withheld due to their personal significance), so I looked up. For the first time in a long time, I heard the Voice of Him in which I thought I worshipped, and it was in my most desperate moment that He spoke to me. I knew it not at the time, but by looking up at what He told me to I momentarily pulled my head away from the gun. This allowed a surreal realization of what I was doing. The seriousness of the situation suddenly flooded my thoughts. I put away the pistol and wept again.

This was not a turning point in any way for me. I still had animosity towards the heavens and was still deeply depressed. I got off the floor, washed my face, walked into my studio room and God spoke again. I look back now and realize the reason why He told me what He did at that precise moment.

I was still a believer in evolution and, due in no small part to that belief, had grown into somewhat of an agnostic. I had never seen God physically (only His creation), the scientists were giving seemingly very convincing arguments against His existence, and He was always silent during my times of distress.

So there I was, a believer in evolution, a drug addict in a deeply depressed state, a growing agnostic who had, literally, just left a room in which I was about to kill myself and God said this, *You will be a preacher.* I had never told God "No" at any time in my life, but at that moment, I not only replied "No!" but I laughed out loud at Him.

Of all the occupations I had ever strove for in life, becoming a preacher was at the very bottom of the list. Here I was with thirty-plus tattoos, an addict with a very bad reputation, hadn't even been inside of a church in some five years or so, and I was going to be a preacher? *Nope.* There was nothing else in the world that I would rather do less, or so I thought. But then, I started thinking about my music. I was working on an album in which I was calling "The Awakening." Perhaps I was to use my music in order to do His work, though I had no plans of changing my style in any way, but maybe I could mention Him a bit more, add an extra "Christian" song here and there, after all, I was a "Christian" still, or so I thought.

My sister wound up coming over to the house a couple of days later. While we were sitting and discussing the recent happenings in our lives, God told me to tell her what He told me. I argued within my spirit, *Why, she's going to think I'm insane?* He urged me, *Tell her.* So I brought it up and her countenance was very similar to my own at first hearing this.

You must understand I was the worst addict in my immediate family. I never went to church and every visible part of my body, including my face, had numerous tattoos scattered upon it. The likelihood of a church becoming comfortable around me was slim-to-none, but standing up before them preaching the good news was impossible to fathom. So I told her about the music idea. She somewhat agreed after that. I was good at music and had a way with lyrics, so that was a possible venture given that I already had a fan base and an audience at my disposal.

A few days later, He told me to say the same thing to my father. The very same reaction took place, but I did what God said and have since realized why He wished for them to hear of what He told me. It was because it was such an unlikely thing to have happen. It was one of the least likely things to take place in our family. The most vulgar individual speaking the words of Jesus - no way, nor was it likely that anyone would listen to them if I spoke. It was to give more witnesses than myself to the miraculous changes God can create in a man's life. God knows the future, He declares the end from the beginning, let this be further proof that He is God and all others are not.

A couple of days later, one of the jobs in which I had applied for called me. Such a relief. My best friend showed up, my ex-girlfriends were coming back around, and my family started calling me. I was ecstatic!

My life seemed to be picking up. But my drug use persisted and, sadly, began to worsen after that. I was experimenting with harder substances (which will go unnamed) and began drinking harder as well. Bacardi 151 became my favorite drink. My music was anything but praise to the Lord, even growing more and more lewd and tawdry with every track.

Around the beginning of 2012, my life of sin was out of control. I was up for doing anything in which would bring pleasure to me: the hardest drugs, women (whether they were married, engaged, it made no difference), harder parties, etc. Many events of this time will be withheld from the reader, but for the people who knew me then, you can testify as to these horrible days.

A few months later in the spring of that year, my new album was finalized and ready for promoting and reviews. The reviews were the best I ever received during all of my fifteen years of making music. I was so thoroughly pleased with this album that I believed this to be my ticket to stardom and riches. Also worth noting around this time was the strong presence of the evil one. I even recorded a momentary time in which he was asking me for my soul in a song called "Adam."

So I took a break from making music while my album was being reviewed and began to read books to pass the time. I loved philosophy, so I read Plato and Henry David Thoreau. I was a fan of Niccolo Machiavelli's *The Prince*, as well as thrillers like Jeffrey Deaver's *Twisted* books and Dante's *Inferno.*

It was during my reading *Inferno* that my interest was directed towards the Bible. The only book in which I should have been reading was the one I shunned the most. What a strange thing to claim to be a Christian and never having a desire to read God's Word. I told myself, "Well, I'll read the New Testament in its entirety. Mom and dad are always talking about the biblical stories, and I, being a supposed Christian should know a bit more about my belief." So I began to read. I had not the slightest inkling that my future was about to be altered in a big way forever.

CHAPTER 6

THE RISE

O merciful Father, in Whom my soul delights. It is this part of my life in which I give total praise to Thee for Your mercy and forgiveness. O blessed Creator of all things, in Whom my soul desires to know more and more, use Your glorious reach in order to guide Your unworthy servant throughout this telling. A blessed amen!

There I was, the summer of 2012, getting high and reading the Bible. Nearly a year it had been since I was in the midst of a crippling depression and wishing death to consume me. Much had transpired since that time, but the best of times were yet to come.

During my reading of the New Testament, I remember telling my parents that I was reading it and sharing some of the things in which I had never known Christ said before. The red letters became so strange and beautiful to me, like the time of my youth. They carried within them wisdom, love, and truth. The great philosophers in whom I had so relied upon for knowledge did not hold such qualities. I kept on reading His words and felt myself growing closer to Him with every verse. I was beginning to understand who the real Jesus Christ was apart from the mental image I had been carrying with me and had tattooed on my body over the past fifteen years.

No other person had said these things. There was no such love to be found in science. No majesty in which could be found in their theories. Everything outside of His words seemed to me cold and stale by comparison. How did I ever set this aside? The One in which I claimed to follow yet rebelled so fervently against. I began to download Christian videos from the internet. I found the video about the apostles from the 1981 movie *Peter and Paul.*

One night in August of 2012, after I had completed my reading of the New Testament, I sparked up and got high as I did every hour or so that I was awake and began watching the movie again. There was something within me that yearned to be like the apostle Paul.

I was still in the midst of promoting my album and was still habitually using drugs and drinking alcohol, but something within me began to stir. About halfway through the movie, I felt strangely moved, convicted even. I ignored the feeling at first, writing it off as a side effect of the drug and nothing more.

The feeling persisted. It was that night that I finally self-examined my own salvation and suddenly, without any warning, realized that I had fallen completely out of fellowship with God and even out of His good grace. I quickly fell to my knees and began the most agonizing prayer in which I will probably ever pray. I wept and wept. I found myself hiding my face in a corner, still crying and begging the Lord for His forgiveness and mercy.

It finally dawned on me that I had left the Lord's will for my own. That I became consumed with what I wanted and not what He wanted. That I was selfish. That I was wretched and full of hatred. I was the exact opposite of everything I was when I was younger and full of faith. I knew that night, at twenty-eight years of age, I needed to repent. I knew not at that moment that I had fallen from grace, but I felt deeply that even after being faithful and saying the sinner's prayer years before, that I was certainly destined for hell.

I fell asleep with tears streaming down my face and awoke to a new day, seemingly the same as any other before it. I used the restroom, washed my faced, brushed my teeth, and then walked back into my studio room. I sat down and reached for my pipe. For the first time in ten-plus years I became suddenly reluctant to smoke from it.

So I put it down and reached for my cigarettes. I lit one up and proceeded to smoke as I had done thousands of times before. About a quarter of the way through it, I put it out without thinking. It suddenly tasted nasty and unsatisfying. I thought there was something wrong with the pack itself, so I put them up for the time.

I gazed back down at the pipe - this was my best friend for the longest time. The thing which had helped me escape so many trials and relieved the stress the world had hurled at me. I picked it up, and put it back down. I remember saying out loud, "I'll see how long I can do without it." I had plenty on hand. I was not running low by any means. I was just reluctant to smoke it for some reason.

So I walked around a bit, and, after an hour or so, took a couple of hits from it. I became anxious, not relaxed. I felt a little guilty and suddenly the buzz was not so enjoyable. Boredom is the usual reason most addicts love to get high. Either that, or because it provides an escape from life. Both of these reasons I have used to justify using drugs.

I slowly began to drift away from getting high. I immediately gave up drinking, but getting high was my greatest obstacle. Sexual desire is the only thing I can compare to my addiction to using. My language immediately cleared up as well. As already stated, I was notorious for my foul language. I now found myself not even willing to speak the lightest of curse words.

About a week after my cry out to the Father, I was under such conviction that I not only ceased from getting high, but I flushed my entire stash. It was nothing easy. I was very reluctant but knew that it was the right thing to do. A few days later, gave up cigarettes. The night I cried out, I asked the Father that if He wished for me to be a preacher, I would, but I needed knowledge. I then asked Him for wisdom.

After I had repented and been made clean, I found myself having an interest in scientific studies. I would study everything from atoms to stars. I also began to research history and biographies of all the greatest scientists. I would stay up all night long, only getting around three hours or so of sleep, because my mind was on my studies. I still have those 3-ring binders that are filled with all types of that knowledge.

Three months after that very crucial night, I was baptized in water at my local church. I believe water baptism to be an important step in growing in grace as it was only after that I began to study the Scriptures and nothing else. All worldly knowledge took a back seat to the spirit world and has done so ever since that day. I began attending church on a regular basis after my baptism, but I had started backsliding. I fell back into getting high, not drinking, not cursing, not fornicating, not partying, but getting high was the one thing which hounded me relentlessly.

One peculiar thing I now realize is that I rarely wished to study while I was high. It was always video games, or movies, or some other nonsense that meant nothing. I repented a few months later, never quitting church, and was once again clean and sober. I would go to church high, though I knew it was wrong and wished not to make a mockery of the Lord. But I had a problem that I was having difficulty shaking.

I found it hard to pray while I was high. The Holy Spirit never failed in letting me know right away what I had to do for that inner peace I once enjoyed to return. I knew without praying, but it became so clear and without excuse while praying.

I did repent and came back shortly after the backsliding period, feeling stronger than ever. The conviction was too much while smoking. I would either give up my sin or give up my fellowship with God - And that wasn't going to happen so long as I could cry out to Him.

After that night of repentance, and over a year and a half afterwards, I still believed in the popularized notion of Once Saved, Always Saved. I would write and study and place all of my focus on the new birth of an individual. My thoughts were on what made up a *true* Christian and how one could be certain that they were a child of God. I believed that a truly reborn Christian who had underwent regeneration and became a true child of the King was destined to heaven in spite of backsliding or falling away from God's will. This, I must say, made backsliding much easier.

Over the next few chapters, I hope to show what I now see as the truth according to the Holy Bible. I once was reluctant in reading many verses in the New Testament pertaining to salvation, but since researching and taking what Jesus said time and time again to heart, I now have no hesitation in reading every verse with clarity and see a picture perfect outline of salvation which is beautiful and without argument. Though, I am not foolish enough to believe that there will be no arguments against the concept of this book, I still feel it worth pointing out what so many millions seem to overlook while reading the Holy Bible. I will now proceed to tell you of what I believe in relation to *true* Eternal Security.

CHAPTER 7

WHAT I BELIEVE

Dearest Father, and Lord of lords, Almighty and Most High God, please guide me throughout this, my sweet Lord! For I love Thee and I know for certain that You love me. Please, O gentle and divine King, give me knowledge and be with Your servant as he attempts to outline the truth in accordance with Your divine and most glorious and eternal Word. Blessed be Your name, amen

This is not an autobiography, but in order for the reader to fully grasp that which I now believe to be the truth, they must first know the extent of my sinful lifestyle under the belief of the popularized *once saved, always saved.*

It was after my thirtieth birthday, in the summer of 2014, that my beliefs began to change in regards to Eternal Security. It was then that I began to write a manuscript. The change occurred while studying the Bible, instead of listening to any man other than Jesus Christ and His apostles, that I now believe very strongly the way that I do.

This book is calling for true Christians to be aloof from this world. Be holy, sober, vigilant, biblically literate, cautious, full of love towards one another, and, above all, be obedient. For with loving obedience to God all of these other attributes will fall into place by themselves.

Let us show first and foremost the danger of taking verses out of context, as most whom follow the popularized O.S.A.S. belief so often do in order to prove their point. I have seen these countless times by such believers.

After they quote certain verses enough, one will come to realize how little else of the Bible they are willing to mention. They overemphasize certain parts. Ask them about abiding faith, bearing fruit, the parables of Christ and their meanings - they mention little else other than those few selected verses in which they cling to and, more often than not, will refuse to hear anything else. It is God's *Word*, not *words*, either take it as a whole or do not take it at all.

Even if they are fairly knowledgeable when it comes to Scripture, they are usually far more stubborn and hardheaded than those who are not.

They may know the story of Moses, Elijah, David, and all of Christ's parables, but they subconsciously tend to skip over the details in relation to salvation in order to feel satisfied and comfortable in their belief.

My point in stating this is that I would have the readers to keep an open mind. I'm not trying to brainwash you, I only ask for your reasoning to be involved while reading what I have to say. This is not a subject to take lightly, in fact, I know of no other subject in which to take more seriously.

Remember how I mentioned to you Satan's greatest trick? I believe that his greatest trick is the way in which he has corrupted the divine truth of Eternal Security. Many may say, "No, he has tricked far more people in more seductive ways than that." I agree, many more people have went to hell over his use of lust, drugs, alcohol, violence, power, prestige, status, greed, all of these things are so obviously of his doing. There's little to no trick involved, only obvious evil in which none of his victims choose to be rid of. But the trickery involved in modern teachings of Once Saved, Always Saved is quite ingenious. It is like a Plan B, of sorts.

Here's the trick as I see it: Be called and convicted by the Holy Spirit, believe in Jesus' name, say the sinner's prayer, confess His name before men, you're saved – no matter what (there's the trick). Water baptism usually follows and that sort of solidifies it for the individual. Little else is done for them, or by them, afterwards. They are assured by many that they are saved, they're going to heaven, so no matter what, they're not going to hell when they die. They go out and usually wind up falling into the same sinful mess they resided in before they were saved.

Some may have even been truly called/convicted, truly believed, truly repented, and were truly within God's grace through true faith at that moment. Yet the trick was already embedded within them. They grow stagnant in their faith. They begin to think that they do not need to act upon the urges to share the gospel, read the Bible, attend church, or be on-fire for God. Their friends are already whispering to one another about how weird they've been acting and their family has been giving them the cold shoulder. The life of sobriety is not so easy to a man with weakened faith, so they begin to allow the trick to settle in thinking, *Ya know, no matter how I live or think, the preacher already said I'm goin' to heaven. I'ma just go back to the old me 'cause I already did all I have to do in order to go to heaven after I die. Sure I won't get rewards, but heaven itself is a great reward. I'll live in the ditch up there so long as I'm not cast into the God's wrath.*

How many times have we all seen someone who has proclaimed to be *saved* go back and forth up to the altar and saying after church, "I just wanted to be sure." That is precisely the problem. There seems to be very little security in the modernized teaching of Eternal Security. Even for those who have truly been reborn, this book is perfect for them. You may be like I was for thirty years, finding it difficult to fully understand certain verses of the Holy Bible in relation to salvation, that's the whole purpose of this book, to clear up all of this confusion and to know what being "saved" truly is.

Before I begin quoting Scripture, I would like to emphasize that I am fully aware that our works cannot save us from our sins. Only true abiding faith in Jesus Christ can ultimately save a person. But here is where the twisting of Bible verses come into play. I'll tell you the truth, as I would rather die than to lie to you.

The deceived are being told that living for Christ is a work, but there is no work on our side involved. Does a deer "work" when he thirsts to the point where he drinks from a pond? Does a person "work" when they awaken in the morning from sleep? These things come naturally as they are only doing what their body urges them to do. The same goes for the spirit. Going to church and obeying the Lord God is only a chore to the deceived or backslidden Christian. The true Christian who abides with the Lord through faithful love has an eagerness and yearning to do His will. Just as the deer thirsts for water, so will our souls for God (Psalm 42). If the deer must cross over an extra hill to reach the water, the crossing over is not seen as "work" but simply a natural action it must take to reach that which sustains its life. It will gladly cross over the hill as its water is there. Because it loves the water, which gives it life, it will do whatever is necessary to reach it and drink from it. So is our love for the LORD; any step in which brings us closer to His presence is not work, but love. God, like the location of the water, does not move. It is the thirst of the deer which drives its steps; it is the Spirit of the LORD which drives ours.

What we see as "works" is no work at all, but comes as naturally as eating, sleeping, breathing, blinking, dreaming and thinking. We do these things not simply because we feel a *need* to, but *want* to. God changes the heart and, by doing so, the body follows with it. That being said let us proceed.

Jesus says clearly in Matthew 24:11, "And many false prophets shall rise, and shall deceive many." The funny thing is, the people who are deceived believe that it is others who are the deceived. It rarely dawns on them that they *are* the deceived.

These same folks have the "itching ears" Paul speaks of in 2 Timothy 4:3,4 and they heap to themselves false prophets and preachers teaching them the easy way of salvation because they will not endure hearing how God's will is central to what every child of His should make their life's ambition. They see the Holy Spirit as a type of ticket into heaven, not as a Comforter or Helper aiding them in their walk of faith and bearing fruit for the kingdom of God. I will now endeavor to tell you the truth from the Word of God in accordance to salvation.

Jesus said in John 15, "I am the true vine, and my Father is the husbandman. Every branch in me that beareth not fruit he taketh away: and every branch that beareth fruit, he purgeth it, that it may bring forth more fruit. Now ye are clean through the word that I have spoken unto you. Abide in me, and I in you. As the branch cannot bear fruit of itself, except it abide in the vine; no more can ye, except ye abide in me. I am the vine, ye are the branches: He that abideth in me, and I in him, the same bringeth forth much fruit: for without me ye can do nothing. If a man abide not in me, he is cast forth as a branch, and is withered; and men gather them, and cast them into the fire, and they are burned. If ye abide in me, and my words abide in you, ye shall ask what ye will, and it shall be done unto you. Herein is my Father glorified, that ye bear much fruit; so shall ye be my disciples. As the Father hath loved me, so have I loved you: continue ye in my love. If ye keep my commandments, ye shall abide in my love; even as I have kept my Father's commandments, and abide in his love... Ye are my friends, if ye do whatsoever I command you."

So Christ is the Vine and we are the branches. He is clearly speaking to the Christians and not to the world. His demand here is quite simple: bear fruit. The penalty for not bearing fruit is stated in verse two, "Every branch in me that beareth not fruit [the Father] taketh away." For all whom believe this to be speaking of merely taking a saved man out of the world before he becomes a stumbling-block, notice what it says in verse five, "I am the vine, ye are the branches: He that abideth in me, and I in him, the same bringeth forth much fruit..." Therefore, one that does not bring forth fruit does *not* abide in Him and is therefore considered outside of the Body of Christ.

Many have asked me what happens when they are reborn; Jesus mentions that in verse 3, "Now ye are clean through the word which I have spoke unto you." That night you are given the power (Holy Spirit) to overcome sin. You are clean and, like the thief on the cross with Christ Jesus, you are deemed worthy for heaven at that moment. It is then that you have faith in Christ and are abiding in Him and willing to do God's will.

He was no longer a servant of sin, but of Christ. Had he lived and fell back into temptation, he would have become the servant of sin again and wondered away from God's will (Romans 6:15,16). Much more elaboration will be given to this crucial subject throughout the rest of this book.

He then goes on with His first instruction after He cleans a person by saying in verse 4, "Abide in me..." meaning walk in the Spirit.

Verse 6 says, "If a man abide not in me, he is cast forth as a branch, and is withered; and men gather them, and cast them into the fire, and they are burned." It is also worth noting that the original Greek word of "abide" here is *meno* that means, "to stay" implying the act of staying with Christ and not going back into the world. By saying "abide" here is implying that they are part of Him; then "cast forth" implies that they are thrown away from Him. My point is that these are not the lost but those whom have been in the Body and not outside of it to begin with.

Once again, it is crucial that people realize that I am not hanging any emphasis on our works. Just as Isaiah 64:6 states, "But we are all as an unclean thing, and all our righteousnesses are as filthy rags..." For it is not our works at all which we are doing after we are reborn, but Christ's work within and through us.

Also important to realize is that I am not implying that sin directly is the reason for one falling from grace. I believe that sin only contributes to the fall as Jesus won the victory over sin by the cross. It is the *heart* of a man that God looks upon; the *soul* of a man which He desires. We all sin. It is possible for a man to sin and his heart to remain with God and arrive in heaven afterwards. But if a man abides in sin for so long that his heart becomes hardened towards God and His conviction, then he no longer serves nor loves God and has become one of Satan's children of disobedience.

The original Greek word of "purgeth" in verse 2 is *kathairo* (kath-ah'-ee-ro) meaning "to cleanse." So God cleanses the saints in which show a willingness to do His will (bear fruit) in order so that He may work more fully through them and, thereby, more of His work may be accomplished. Remember He says in this same chapter, "...for without me ye can do nothing."

Jesus works through us upon the new birth. It is therefore His works that are being done, not ours. For we are crucified to the world, and the world to us (Galatians 6:14). It is no longer us that live, but Christ living within us and working through us (Philippians 1:21).

What happens to the branches (those whom are in the Body of Christ) that do not bear fruit (do His will)? They are thrown out, wither, men gather them up, cast them into the fire and they are burned (verse 6). In referring to verses 7-10: How do we become His disciples? By bearing fruit. What is He demanding?

For us to continue in His love. How do we continue (or abide) in His love? By keeping His commandments.

The importance of fruit bearing is also illustrated in the parable of the wicked tenants in Matthew 21. Jesus states in verse 43, "Therefore say I unto you, The kingdom of God shall be taken from you, and given to a nation bringing forth the fruits thereof." He says this referencing the kingdom being taken from the Jews and given unto the Gentiles, this due to their disobedience to God, not for their lack of profession and/or ritual keeping, but disobedience, as they were quick to profess God and attempt to live for Him, but only in the sight of men so that they could be elevated and praised. For it is written, "This people draweth nigh unto me with their mouth, and honoureth me with their lips; but their heart is far from me." The fruit is proof of the heart.

My good friend and Pastor once told me that Jesus Christ is like our boss or employer. If we are under the lordship of someone on this earth, we obey them. The penalty for not obeying the boss is termination of employment. Why should it be any different for our relationship with God? If He gives us a job to do, like a normal boss would do, why do we think it alright to disobey the Lord of lords and King of kings and remain within His good graces? The answer is obvious and pointed out in Luke 6:46 by Jesus Himself.

The same could be said of a father/son relationship. How long would a good father allow a disobedient son to remain in his home? The fallen angels were once called sons of God and resided with the good Father in His home, that is, until they became disobedient. They were then, as we all know, banished from His presence forever.

We err in thinking that there is no sacrifice on our part. The way of salvation is grounded in sacrifice: God gave His Son; Jesus gave His blood; we give our *all* in return. You've heard it said that Jesus doesn't want a part-time Christian, this is true. We are told to first deny ourselves, take up our cross and follow Him (Matthew 16:24), to die daily, to become the new man and do away with the old. Jesus Christ Himself even takes it a step further by saying in Matthew 10:38, "And he that taketh not his cross, and followeth after me, is not worthy of me." Only the deceived at heart take these commandments lightly.

1 John 2:3,4 states, "And hereby we do know that we know him, if we keep his commandments. He that saith, I know him, and keepeth not his commandments, is a liar, and the truth is not in him." So anyone not keeping the commandments of God, which is to be holy, righteous, and obedient, does not know Him. They who say they are Christians, yet do not obey His commandments are liars, and the truth is not in them.

1 John 3:24 also speaks of this, "And he that keepeth his commandments dwelleth in him. And hereby we know that he abideth in us, by the Spirit which he hath given us." Again, a clear statement of keeping God's commandments being a showing of those whom dwell within the Body of Christ. When you see an individual keeping the commandments of God there is good fruit, therefore, that individual has the Holy Spirit inhabiting their temple.

1 John 5:3, "For this is the love of God, that we keep his commandments: and his commandments are not grievous." God's love for us and our love for God go hand-in-hand with keeping His commandments. He is the Government of our lives upon accepting Christ as our Savior; no others will matters than His will, not even our own.

Jesus says in John 14:21, "He that hath my commandments, and keepeth them, he it is that loveth me: and he that loveth me shall be loved of my Father, and I will love him, and will manifest myself to him." This He spoke of the Holy Spirit that I will attempt to get into further detail later on in this book (Lord willing).

So obedience seems to be of great importance to God. What does the apostle Paul call the sinners of the world in Ephesians 2:2, "Wherein in time past ye walked according to the course of this world, according to the prince of the power of the air, the spirit that now worketh in the children of disobedience:" So, if Satan's followers are labeled "children of disobedience" then God's children must be seen as children of obedience, right. Notice, they're not called, *children who didn't say the prayer at the altar one night* but are simply labeled "children of disobedience." I speak not of disobedience being because they sin, but because they are unfaithful. It is the absence of faith that causes one's fall from grace, as we are saved by grace through faith.

Jesus says in John 8:31,32, "If ye continue in my word, then ye are my disciples indeed; And ye shall know the truth, and the truth shall make you free." Here, He clearly states again what must be done in order to be His disciple - to continue in His Word. He then goes on in verses 34,35, "Verily, verily, I say unto you, Whosoever committeth sin is the servant of sin. And the servant abideth not in the house for ever: but the Son abideth ever."

Jesus says (verses 34,35) that whosoever commits sin is the servant of sin (and, therefore, not a child of God). One may then read Romans 6:16, "Know ye not, that to whom ye yield yourselves servants to obey, his servants ye are to whom ye obey; whether of sin unto death, or of obedience unto righteousness."

Ecclesiastes 12:13, Solomon, the wisest man (besides Jesus Christ) to ever live, stated the conclusion to his observance of life: "Fear God, and keep his commandments: for this is the whole duty of man." Ironically, many believe that because we are under grace now, we are granted more liberties to do what we want to do, in all actuality, nothing could be further from the truth. We are granted the Comforter that helps us discern what is right from what is wrong. God has made His temple our bodies, we are therefore expected to keep it holy at all times.

Jesus said in Matthew 5:20, "For I say unto you, That except your righteousness shall exceed the righteousness of the scribes and Pharisees, ye shall in no case enter into the kingdom of heaven." I am well aware that our righteousness is Jesus Christ within us. What Christ says here is if He is found within us, then we are counted as righteous before the Father.

The reason I bring this verse up is to state that Jesus was perfect and acceptable in God's presence. That very same perfect and holy Being lives inside of each believer. He guides us throughout our daily walk. He convicts us whenever we sin. He is our Comforter in times of distress. My point is that if this Spirit lives within a man, His guidance, convicting power, and comforting presence will reside within each of those who are within His grace. If an individual has not these things, then they must not have His Spirit and, thereby, not His grace.

How can a man be the light of the world and dwell in darkness for days without number?

How often have backslidden Christians, even preachers, said, "Well, we're all only human" or "Nobody's perfect..." to justify their sinful lives. Why then are we called *saints?* Children of God do not live sinful lives. A set apart people are called "separate" (holy) because they are not like the world. Such wolves wink at sin as if it's a game. Beware of such men. I have known many pastors who are the weakest spiritual men in the church. Does it not state in Leviticus 19:2 and 1 Peter 1:16, "Be ye holy; for I am holy."

Who is it that inhabits a person upon the rebirth? The Holy Spirit. The Holy Spirit is far stronger than those whom He inhabits, but the man must do as Paul states in 1 Corinthians 15:31, "die daily" to himself in order so that the Holy Spirit may do His work through him. Just as John the Baptist says in John 3:30, "He must increase, but I must decrease."

I heard it once said, "The Holy Spirit makes holy people who live holy lives." Anyone who says anything of the contrary is of the devil and has no part, nor place, with God.

Proverbs 14:14 says, "The backslider in heart shall be filled with his own ways: and a good man shall be satisfied from himself." This verse alone defines the lifestyle of a backslider. They will do what pleases them while a man of God will say, "Thy will be done."

There is the worldly man, and the Godly man – there are no other types in this world.

When Isaiah sees the LORD in His tabernacle in Isaiah 6, the fiery seraphims are crying, "holy, holy, holy is the LORD of hosts," the same is revealed by Jesus Christ to John in the book of Revelation. My point is that God never changes. He is always holy. Man changes many times, in many ways, in few days. The Holy Spirit is the Comforter that helps the man change - sometimes slowly, sometimes quickly - into a holy man, acceptable to God through Jesus Christ.

The change must be one in which the man agrees to; something not forced upon him. As the old saying goes, *A man convinced against his will, is under the same opinion still*, meaning that if it is not a willing acceptance of holiness on the man's part, be it on this earth or in heaven, he will not be in the presence of God. God is holy and only those who are found within His Son, and willingly walking in the Spirit, will be in His presence forever.

Worth noting also is what Paul states in Titus 1:8, instructing Titus on the characteristics of a bishop of God, "[Be a] lover of hospitality, a lover of good men, sober, just, holy, temperate;" There are a couple of things which can be gathered from this: the mentioning of good men and the mentioning of being holy (which is also disputed as being impossible while in this life).

This is not a way for me to emphasize works, but works are a showing of what is within a man's heart. God sees the heart. Jesus said that we would know the followers of Him by their fruits (or works). This is why I am writing this book. Who is within your heart? Who do you truly follow? Who is Lord?

Many preachers have I heard say to their congregations, "No matter what you do, your sins are forgiven - past, present, and future." or "You may forsake God, but He'll never forsake you." Why then does it say in 1 Corinthians 6:9,10, "Know ye not that the unrighteous shall not inherit the kingdom of God? Be not deceived: neither fornicators, nor idolaters, nor adulterers, nor effeminate, nor abusers of themselves with mankind, nor thieves, nor covetous, nor drunkards, nor revilers, nor extortioners, shall inherit the kingdom of God."

Many may try to argue this away as being solely for the outright sinners, and claim something very foolish as, "Well, that doesn't apply to Christians." So Christians are allowed to do such things? Preposterous!

Why then does it say in 1 John 2:15-17, "Love not the world, neither the things that are in the world. If any man love the world, the love of the Father is not in him. For all that is in the world, the lust of the flesh, and the lust of the eyes, and the pride of life, is not of the Father, but is of the world. And the world passeth away, and the lust thereof: but he that doeth the will of God abideth for ever."

There it says it again, "...he that doeth the will of God..." Another verse clearly stating that doing the will of the Father is all-important and crucial. In John 8:29, Jesus says, "And he that sent me is with me: the Father hath not left me alone; for I do always those things that please him." Again, we see that Jesus Himself did the will of the Father.

Notice how Christ lived in the Father's will and was said of the Father, "This is my beloved Son, in whom I am well pleased" (Matthew 17:5). Satan was found to have iniquity within him (Ezekial 28:15), and was therefore cast out of heaven and away from God's presence.

Why am I stressing this, you may be asking. Because we err in thinking that our hearts can't be led astray, and away from grace, when we fall into a sinful lifestyle. So many in which cling to the popularized O.S.A.S. belief are out there committing just a many sins as before, if not more, thinking that they're going to heaven when they die regardless of how many sins they commit along the way.

I am not stating that we can live sinless lives, but we must walk within the Spirit of God and not let our hearts be misled in believing that sin is such a non-issue once we are reborn. Sin can lead one right back into their old lives and lead one's heart away from grace if given enough leeway. Be sober and vigilant!

CHAPTER 8

BACKSLIDING

*Almighty Father, Lord of all things, blessed
art Thou above the stars and galaxies in
which surround us. O mighty God, please
hear your servant's prayer to You. I seek
only to do Thy will and not my will. Have
these things only be done if Thou would
have them be done. May this work glorify
You and only You, dear God! Amen!*

If ever there was a supposed *get out of jail free* card in
which all the sinners whom cling to Eternal Security
love to play everyday, it's this one - *backsliding*. This
word means about as much to the people doing it as
burning the bacon in the morning. Such apathy over
a serious act is so scary that no words in which I could
conjure up would be sufficient in defining it.

This is grace: Because of Christ's blood, every
man, both Jew and Gentile are to walk by faith to

obtain the righteousness of Christ Jesus, the spotless Lamb of God. To be free with Jesus as our Mediator instead of enslaved and in bondage by the Law of Moses. We are now to be judged based upon whether we accept Christ as Lord, instead of cursed by default by the law. It is our reliance on God the Son instead of self that is now the only way to heaven as all things have been placed under His dominion.

The Gentiles are now able to come into the fold of the Jewish people and we can all be one in Christ Jesus. We are all now given the opportunity to know God through the Holy Spirit in Whom aids us in our walk of serving the Lord and doing His will. Remember the book of Ruth - how Boaz was a type of Christ, and Ruth was a Gentile woman allowed into his field and wound up marrying him.

I know this story actually happened, but there is great symbology involved here: Ruth represents Gentiles; Boaz represents Christ; His field represents God's grace. We are allowed into His grace because He sees us in need, humbled, and admitting our need of salvation.

My point in stating these things is that though we are not under the law but grace, He consistently calls out for us to repent. Why? Because, just like the Jews of old, we will die with reprobate hearts that we have either knowingly or ignorantly turned away from God, for it is the heart that is seen and not the flesh.

That is the seriousness of backsliding. I do believe that a man can fall out of the grace of God. Without grace, there is no entering into His kingdom. We will deal more with the subject of salvation in the next few chapters.

Time and time again throughout the Old Testament, Israel was backsliding. And God would strike them over their iniquities in an attempt to bring them back. We care not to use the word when speaking of our own country - "America is backsliding" - We just hesitate to use it in relation to ourselves. Even then, those who believe in *once saved, always saved* pay very little heed to their backsliding. Grace is always overemphasized with them, yet there are verses such as Galatians 5:7, "Ye did run well: who did hinder you that ye should not obey the truth?" Notice the wording Paul uses here – *"obey the truth"* signifying obedience to the truth of God. Not a simple acknowledging of the truth, but obedience to it.

They trust that God will be merciful to them because, hey, they believe in Jesus Christ and prayed for Him to come into their hearts and save them one night. Sure, they may callously sin regularly without conviction or repentance, but everybody does and not everybody is going to hell, right? Let us first look at some verses in Hebrews 10 in order to gather from Scripture what the answer to such questions may be.

Hebrews 10:23,24 - "Let us hold fast the profession of our faith, having our hearts sprinkled from an evil conscience, and our bodies washed with pure water. Let us hold fast the profession of our faith without wavering; (for he is faithful that promised;) And let us consider one another to provoke unto love and to good works:"

Verses 23 and 24 begin with encouraging the believers in Jesus Christ to hold fast their professions of faith. Verse 24 emphasizes this point by adding, "*without wavering.*" Obviously, faith is of the utmost importance in our salvation.

We are saved "by grace, through faith" (Ephesians 2:8), but faith is not a momentary thing which is to be exercised in one night alone, or for only a short time, then, afterwards, set aside for the things of the world. It is an ongoing characteristic in the Christian life. Those with faith know that, like sanctification, it is an ongoing process throughout the life of a Christian. Further elaboration on this will be listed in later chapters.

Let us look at the verses in the Word of God once again to clarify what it says of who is part of the Body of Christ: Matthew 12:50, "For whosoever shall do the will of my Father which is in heaven the same is my brother, and sister, and mother." To do the will of God is the most emphasized mission in the whole Bible. Nothing else even comes close to being more important. Not following God's will (which includes believing in His Son) is always followed by His wrath. Sin is transgression against God. Hebrews 10 is a telling chapter for all those who fall back into sin and/ or cease from doing God's will.

Hebrews 10:25 - "Not forsaking the assembling of ourselves together, as the manner of some is; but exhorting one another: and so much the more, as ye see the day approaching." I know of many supposed Christians who do not even attend church as they have been told time and time again that it is not a requirement to get into heaven. But does Jesus not say in Luke 11:23, "He that is not with me is against me: and he that gathereth not with me scattereth."

Obeying God's commandments are crucial and it is biblical in stating that if one desires to do the Lord's will, (one of which is to attend church; verse 25), and exhorting others (the best place to do so is in the assembly), in wishing to do these things, you will know that you are His disciple and a child of God (2 John 6).

The verses in which I would say are very blatant concerning one whom backslides are verses 26 and 27, "For if we sin wilfully after that we have received the knowledge of the truth, there remaineth no more sacrifices for sin, but a certain fearful looking for of judgment and fiery indignation, which shall devour the adversaries."

So let's take this slowly: It is written, "For if we sin wilfully after that we have received the knowledge of the truth" meaning what it says; That if our will turns from God to sin, after receiving the gospel and hearing the good Word, then, "there remaineth no more sacrifices for sin..." Meaning that no other way can be found to sanctify us from sin and to justify us before God than through the cross of our Lord and Savior Jesus Christ, which has at that point been forfeited.

But many have said that *every* sin is a willful sin, but this is not true. There are certain things that can happen that are out of our control, such as dreams, certain demonically directed thoughts, accidently stumbling across a godless action in a movie without prior knowledge. Remember, this world is working against us, as well as the flesh, as well as the devil himself. There are many things in which are out of our control which are placed in front of us on a daily basis. We can minimize such things but there will always be temptations and things not of God used to take us from Him while on this earth.

Hebrews 10:28-31 compares the penalty for transgressing the law of Moses and the new covenant of the Spirit of grace: "He that despised Moses' law died without mercy under two or three witnesses: Of how much sorer punishment, suppose ye, shall he be thought worthy, who hath trodden under foot the Son of God, and hath counted the blood of the covenant, wherewith he was sanctified, an unholy thing, and hath done despite unto the Spirit of grace? For we know him that hath said, Vengeance belongeth unto me, I will recompense, saith the Lord. And again, The Lord shall judge his people. It is a fearful thing to fall into the hands of the living God."

Verse 29 is quite terrifying, as it is speaking to the reborn Christian and not to the world: "Of how much sorer punishment, suppose ye, shall he be thought worthy, who hath trodden under foot the Son of God, and hath counted the blood of the covenant, wherewith he was sanctified, an unholy thing, and hath done despite unto the Spirit of grace?" In this the author of Hebrews is declaring a greater punishment will be upon him who makes a mockery of the Son of God and the sacrifice He had to give in order to justify us before the Father. This is a clear indication that the author is addressing one whom has been born again, as sanctification has already began its progression, and has been "trodden under foot" by the individual in whom the holy work was done.

The original Greek word here for "despite" is *enubrizo* (en-oo-brid'-zo) meaning, "to insult." So this person's act is an insult to the Spirit of grace, which is the reasoning behind the greater punishment.

Hebrews 10:32-34 - "But call to remembrance the former days, in which, after ye were illuminated, ye endured a great flight of afflictions; Partly whilst ye were made a gazingstock both by reproaches and afflictions; and partly, whilst ye became companions of them that were so used. For ye had compassion of me in my bonds, and took joyfully the spoiling of your goods, knowing in yourselves that ye have in heaven a better and an enduring substance."

Verse 32 is encouraging the reader to remember the days when they were first made new and enlightened by the Holy Spirit. It brings into remembrance all the trials and tribulations in which the newly reborn believer had overcome in Christ's name. Verse 33 begins to name the trials that were overcome. Verse 34 states the reward in which is building in heavenly places, even though all the earthly possessions are fading away upon accepting Jesus Christ as Savior.

Hebrews 10:35,36 - "Cast not away therefore your confidence, which hath great recompence of reward. For ye have need of patience, that, after ye have done the will of God, ye might receive the promise." What is our confidence (verse 35)? Our great hope, which is from faith in Jesus Christ, which carries a great reward. Patience is then brought up (verse 36) and the promise of the great reward comes after we have done the will of God.

Hebrews 10:38,39 - "Now the just shall live by faith: but if any man draw back, my soul shall have no pleasure in him. But we are not of them who draw back unto perdition; but of them that believe to the saving of the soul." Verse 38 begins with the author quoting Habakkuk 2:4, "Now the just shall live by faith."

It then goes on, "but if any man *draw back"* - clearly implying that it is possible for one to backslide away from faith, and, ultimately, the will of God - "my soul shall have *no pleasure* in him."

The author then goes on in verse 39 with something very telling indeed, "But we are not of them who draw back *unto perdition;"* This is stating a petrifying thing - that those who steer away from God's will no longer have abiding faith in Christ and, becoming backsliders, are destined for perdition (which is hell).

He then concludes the chapter with, "but of them that believe to the saving of the soul." This is stating that we must have ongoing and abiding faith, not a temporary sort. I will relate back to the significance of what this implies in later chapters to show my final point in regards to the truth of Eternal Security.

All who live under the law are cursed as they are all found guilty of transgressions against God (Galatians 3:10). Galatians 5:18-21 says, "But if ye be led of the Spirit, ye are not under the law. Now the works of the flesh are manifest, which are these; Adultery, fornication, uncleanness, lasciviousness, idolatry, witchcraft, hatred, variance, emulations, wrath, strife, seditions, heresies, envyings, murders, drunkenness, revellings, and such like: of the which I tell you before, as I have also told you in time past, that they which do such things shall not inherit the kingdom of God."

He then gives the characteristics of them who do abide in faith, verses 22-24, "But the fruit of the Spirit is love, joy, peace, longsuffering, gentleness, goodness, faith, meekness, temperance: against such there is no law. And they that are Christ's have crucified the flesh with the affections and lusts."

Many have pointed out the story of the Prodigal Son found in Luke 15:11-32 to support their stance on being "saved" at the time of saying the sinner's prayer. The story goes as thus:

"A certain man had two sons: And the younger of them said to his father, Father, give me the portion of goods that falleth to me. And he divided unto them his living. And not many days after the younger son gathered all together, and took his journey into a far country, and there wasted his substance with riotous living. And when he had spent all, there arose a mighty famine in that land; and he began to be in want. And he went and joined himself to a citizen of that country; and he sent him into his fields to feed swine. And he would fain have filled his belly with the husks that the swine did eat: and no man gave unto him. And when he came to himself, he said, How many hired servants of my father's have bread enough and to spare, and

I perish with hunger! I will arise and go to my father, and will say unto him, Father, I have sinned against heaven, and before thee, And am no more worthy to be called thy son: make me as one of thy hired servants. And he arose, and came to his father. But when he was yet a great way off, his father saw him, and had compassion, and ran, and fell on his neck, and kissed him. And the son said unto him, Father, I have sinned against heaven, and in thy sight, and am no more worthy to be called thy son. But the father said to his servants, Bring forth the best robe, and put it on him; and put a ring on his hand, and shoes on his feet: And bring hither the fatted calf, and kill it; and let us eat, and be merry: For this my son was dead, and is alive again; he was lost, and is found. And they began to be merry. Now his elder son was in the field: and as he came and drew nigh to the house, he heard musick and dancing. And he called one of the servants, and asked what these things meant. And he said unto him, Thy brother is come; and thy father hath killed the fatted calf, because he hath received him safe and sound. And he was angry, and would not go in: therefore came his father out, and intreated him. And he answering said to his father, Lo, these many years do I serve thee, neither transgressed I at any time thy commandment: and yet thou never gavest me a kid, that I might make merry with my friends: But as soon as this thy son was come, which hath devoured thy living with harlots, thou hast killed for him the fatted calf. And he said unto him, Son, thou art ever with me, and all that I have is thine. It was meet that we should make merry, and be glad: for this thy brother was dead, and is alive again; and was lost, and is found."

One of the most intelligent preachers I have ever heard (a firm believer in the popularized *once saved, always saved*) used this story as one of his points of proof to his belief. He stated something to this effect, "Well, yeah, the son sinned, left his father, and squandered his inheritance, but he was still the father's son." This angers me so much that I am flabbergasted. It's as if he (and others like him) completely overlooked every point that is made in the parable by Jesus Christ, except the parts in which supports his belief.

First off, let's begin with putting this story into context. In the verses before it, Jesus is speaking of the joy over a sinner (or, more specifically, backslider) who comes to repentance. He states in 15:4, "What man of you, having an hundred sheep, if he lose one of them, doth not leave the ninety and nine in the wilderness, and go after that which is lost, until he find it?" He then states in 15:8, "Either what woman having ten pieces of silver, if she lose one piece, doth not light a candle, and sweep the house, and seek diligently till she find it?"

Let's think logically, for both the man whom lost his sheep, and the woman whom lost her coin, to have lost them, they would have had to own them in the first place. Just as one would already have to be within the fold of Christ, so would the sheep and coin have to already be in the possession of the man and woman before they could lose them.

We are not born into being children of God, but children of Adam. We must come into the fold of God's mercy and find grace in His sight, right? So, by the story centering on the father's son instead of a stranger is very telling. It is implying that the son is already under the wing of the father, just as a reborn individual is under the wing of Christ and the Father God.

The story is that of a backslider, not a sinner whom has never known God beforehand. As I just stated, this is a son, not a servant or stranger who does not know the father, but a son. They know one another intimately, not just by hearsay.

Jesus says to the sheep after they have finally been divided from the goats in Matthew 25:34, "Come, ye blessed of my Father, inherit the kingdom prepared for you from the foundation of the world." It is after this world has passed that the inheritance is given to the children of God, not while we are in it. Meaning, only upon death will we receive our inheritance. But the Prodigal Son wishes to take his inheritance early (a sign of selfishness, impatience, and disobedience - everything in which is advised against for the faithful), in other words, he backslides and wishes to do his own will and not the father's.

After he squanders everything, which is representative of life without Christ, he then "came to himself" and knew to repent and return to the father. Upon his return, his brother is angry with his father. The reason that he gives is very telling. He says, "Lo, these many years do I *serve* thee, neither *transgressed* I at any time thy commandment" which is what his younger brother did.

Remember when the Prodigal Son says, "I have sinned against heaven, and in thy sight..." His sin was that he no longer wished to serve the father and do what his father willed. He went against his father's commandment, became impatient and took his inheritance prematurely and squandered it.

The most telling part of this entire story is the father's reply upon celebrating his son's return. Keep in mind now what the argument here was from the intelligent preacher I mentioned earlier: that the son was still the father's son, even though he left his father and squandered his inheritance; implying that if one is reborn and becomes a child of God, then no sin will ever take away their status as God's child - which is the modern-day teaching of Eternal Security.

Upon the Prodigal Son's return, the father celebrates. His reason for celebrating was said in this way, "For this my son was *dead*, and is alive again; he was *lost*, and is found." This is incredibly telling of those whom choose to go from God into the world. Jesus says, "I am life" (John 14:6), all those not within the Body of Christ are therefore dead. I believe that to be the reason why everlasting separation from Him is called the second death, but that is another topic for another time.

So while the son was away, he was *dead*, and *lost*, to the father. This is a symbolic meaning, of course, one in which is of a spiritual nature. The son was alive, and safe, while with the father; he was dead, and lost, when he left the father and went outside of his father's will. So what would have happened had the son have died while out in the world and not with his father? He would have died in the world, with the world; he would not have died under his father's wing. Therefore, his fate would have been the same as those in the world.

Also worth noting is what God said in Malachi 2:17,18, "And they shall be mine, saith the LORD of hosts, in that day when I make up my jewels; and I will spare them, as a man spareth his own son that serveth him. Then shall ye return, and discern between the righteous and the wicked, between him that serveth God and him that serveth him not."

Notice how God mentions his son and serving Him in the same manner. Like the elder son (in verse 29), those whom serve Him are spared and favored; but those whom do not serve Him (whether once labeled a son or not) are deemed "*wicked.*"

2 Corinthians 5:15, Paul speaks of the relationship between Christ and the followers, saying, "And that he died for all, that they which live should not henceforth live unto themselves, but unto him which died for them, and rose again." Obviously, Paul is emphasizing the importance of living for the Lord and no longer for self. This does beg the question (in which I am attempting to address) as to what happens if one does begin to live for themselves after they have lived for God?

1 Corinthians 5:11,13, Paul is addressing a situation in the church of Corinth, he says, "But now I have written unto you not to keep company, if any man that is called a brother be a fornicator, or covetous, or an idolater, or a railer, or a drunkard, or an extortioner... put away from among yourselves that wicked person."

The primary reason for me quoting these verses is to point out that Paul calls the man in question a "brother" meaning one saying that he's a Christian. Whether he truly is or not is beside the point, the fact is that Paul says to none-the-less, if he is a "wicked" man, Christian or not, to not congregate with him;

implying that he has no part nor place with God and other Christians.

Romans 8:5-8, "For they that are after the flesh do mind the things of the flesh; but they that are after the Spirit the things of the Spirit. For to be carnally minded is death; but to be spiritually minded is life and peace. Because the carnal mind is enmity against God: for it is not subject to the law of God, neither indeed can be. So then they that are in the flesh cannot please God."

Notice how it is written that being carnally *minded* is death. How many professing Christians are there which we see paying far more heed to the world than to God? They are more fixated on their television programs or vehicles or sports than on serving the Lord God.

Paul then goes on in verse 13, "For if ye live after the flesh, ye shall die: but if ye through the Spirit do mortify the deeds of the body, ye shall live." This is so fervently attacking those whom live in the flesh, but verse 13 is the most telling in stating the penalty for living after the flesh - *death*; but for those who put away their fleshly desires - *life*. For those of whom say this to mean that the *death* mentioned here is that of the physical body and not of the spiritual, may I remind you that all physical bodies are appointed to die once (Hebrews 9:27), therefore, this death is that of a spiritual nature as Paul is speaking of a distinction between those who die and those who live. Paul physically died, does that mean that he lived after the flesh in sin?

Christ said in Luke 9:62, "No man, having put his hand to the plough, and looking back, is fit for the kingdom of God." So Jesus is saying that not just anybody can enter into heaven, only those who cease from turning back to their old ways (repent) are deemed worthy of entering the pearly gates.

This is more solidified in Christ's words of Luke 17:32 when He simply states, "Remember Lot's wife."

In Genesis 19, the death of Lot's wife is written. God declares destruction on the city of Sodom and the angels sought about saving Lot, his two daughters, and his wife. The story is true, but also symbolic in many ways. His family begins to enter into the city of Zoar while destruction was raining down upon the sinful city of Sodom. They were given specific instructions to not look back on the city of sin in order for their souls to be saved (see verse 20), but Lot's wife goes against God's will, looks back on her old life, and is stricken with the same level of punishment as those within the city (verse 26). A telling thing.

Backsliding has always been a dangerous thing. In Numbers 15, we can see that for those who sin ignorantly are shown great mercy, but the soul who is found to sin knowingly is (as verse 31 states) "...cut off; his iniquity shall be upon him."

In verses 39 & 40, God's people are commanded to "...remember all the commandments of the LORD, and do them; and that ye seek not after your own heart and your own eyes, after which ye used to go a whoring: That ye may remember, and do all my commandments, and be holy unto your God." Once again, God has always commanded holiness from His children.

Much of what I believe to be happening today can be illustrated in Isaiah 4:1, "And in that day seven women shall take hold of one man, saying, We will eat our own bread, and wear our own apparel: only let us be called by thy name, to take away our reproach." Many even born-again Christians are turning into such as these women when they become lukewarm, begin disobeying the Lord, and use Christ's name in order to not feel a coming reproach for becoming sinful again. A perfect illustration.

There are two verses I wish to quickly cite in order to show the judgment upon the wicked: 1 Corinthians 11:32, Paul states, "But when we are judged, we are chastened of the Lord, that we should not be condemned with the world." The word "condemned" here in the original Greek is *katakrino* (kat-ak-ree'-no) meaning, "to judge against, i.e. sentence" the only alternative word given is "damn." So, it means damnation, right?

Skip ahead to the second verse in James 5:9, "Grudge not one against another, brethren, lest ye be condemned: behold, the judge standeth before the door." Notice who he is addressing, the brethren, these are the ones who are in the Body of Jesus Christ - the Christians, not the lost. He exhorts them to not hold grudges as they then run the risk of being condemned (or damned). This goes back to what Jesus Christ said of forgiving one another being a requirement of the Father's forgiveness towards us (Mark 11:25,26).

My point in citing these two verses is that there is great ignorance in assuming that belief (and nothing else, i.e. repentance, which accompanies *the* faith; which carries with it the bearing of good fruit) is the only requirement for one to be justified before the Father in Christ Jesus.

In 2 Peter 3:17,18 it is written, "Ye therefore, beloved, seeing ye know these things before, beware lest ye also, being led away with the error of the wicked, fall from your own stedfastness. But grow in grace, and in the knowledge of our Lord and Saviour Jesus Christ..." The disciple is warning the brethren to beware of the ways of the wicked, which brings about the consequence of falling from headstrong continuance in the Lord. This may not seem like such a big deal in accordance to what I'm speaking on until you get to verse 18, which begins with Simon Peter exhorting the brethren to *grow in grace.*

So, like faith, grace is something in which one can grow. If one can grow in grace, like faith, then one can also find that grace can ultimately be found completely lacking in regards to the backsliding individual; that is, if the person remains in such a state, in which case, only God can be the judge.

Revelation 2:4,5, Jesus says to the church of the Ephesians (but to His Church, in general), "Nevertheless I have somewhat against thee, because thou hast left thy first love. Remember therefore from whence thou art fallen, and repent, and do the first works; or else I will come unto thee quickly, and I will remove thy candlestick out of his place, except thou repent." This mentions not only the possibility of falling from our first Love (Christ), but also the penalty for not repenting, which is the removal of such individuals.

Backsliders have a nasty habit of using God to live comfortably in sin; the true Christian will strive to avoid sin, while at the same time allowing God to use them. It is a life of servitude, for both a child, and servant alike, obedience is demanded, not suggested.

1 Corinthians 3:16,17, "Know ye not that ye are the temple of God, and that the Spirit of God dwelleth in you? If any man defile the temple of God, him shall God destroy; for the temple of God is holy, which

temple ye are." Many would say this advocates the preaching of God destroying a man's body alone, but notice that it says "*him* shall God destroy" not merely his body, but *him* altogether is the implication. Just as the Uzzah was destroyed when he touched the holy ark of God due to him being sinful, so is the soul that sins destroyed when found defiling the temple of God, which is the body of His children on earth.

But the story of Uzzah is a one in which the LORD's timing in judgment can be viewed. You see, before Uzzah was killed immediately for defiling the ark of God, the Philistines had captured it and put it in a celebratory fashion in front of their god Dagon (1 Samuel 5). This did not invoke God's wrath immediately, due to the fact that the Philistines had very little knowledge of God, whereas Uzzah had a greater knowledge of God and His severity. The same goes for the backslider in contrast with the outright sinner. The backslider has a greater understanding of what God commands so is thereby held to a higher accountability and standard – both in regards to obedience, as well as in punishment for disobedience. God will, most of the time, extend His mercy to those lacking in knowledge and understanding of Him. So if you are confused as to why God isn't punishing the backslider or outright sinner, worry not, let this be a showing of God's greater judgment in mercy as He knows fully well the consequence of the unrepentant soul.

I will end this chapter by quoting the apostle Paul in his letter to the Galatians. Galatians 2:17,18 says, "But if, while we seek to be justified by Christ, we ourselves also are found sinners, is therefore Christ the minister of sin? God forbid. For if I build again the things which I destroyed, I make myself a transgressor." Paul states, "While we seek to be justified," this is mentioning the importance of steadfast faith and on-going repentance being of great importance in accordance to salvation.

The original Greek word for "transgressor" there is *parabates* (par-ab-at'-ace) defined as "a violator." John speaks of transgressors in 2 John 9, "Whosoever transgresseth, and abideth not in the doctrine of Christ hath not God..."

There are no violators in heaven, the last that I knew were deemed violators of God's will are now not allowed into heaven. The first to say, "I will" (Isaiah 14:12-14) while in the presence of God was thrown out, away from His presence afterwards. The backslider, until they repent, does the same. Why should a faithless man who was once faithful be viewed in a different manner? It is a privilege to spend an eternity with God. Only those whose hearts are with Him, and happily serve Him are deemed worthy of such a privilege.

CHAPTER 9

FAITH

My God and love of my life, dear Father, it is Thy in Whom I adore over all things! Please O precious heavenly Maker, let it be known of how Your servant serves only You and no other. O how I cherish Your presence, dear Lord of my life! Lead me now, and give unto the beholder of these things knowledge in which they might discernment what is that good and faithful Word! Amen

Faith is the most essential quality that a Christian can possibly possess. I used to take it so lightly, but, as I grow in the Word of God, I can see how it is of the greatest importance! It is written, "...without faith it is impossible to please him..."

There are two forms in which make up true faith: *intellectual* and *inward*. Many believe with the mind, but not with the heart. Only the Father can change the heart and only until He calls one to come to Him will they even be able to have the second (inward) faith enacted. It is the Holy Ghost in which is the inward change. I believe Romans 10:9,10 are great verses to cite for proof of this being *the* faith.

Intellectual faith is the individual believing with the mind and confessing with the mouth; many have this kind of faith. *Inward* faith is the conviction and comfort in which the Holy Spirit plays a significant role in helping the individual have a change of heart (*"unto righteousness"*), which is to be more like Christ. These two breed the fear, love, trust and fellowship of the Lord.

The outward showing of truly having *the* faith is the natural overflow of these two kinds being made manifest within the individual through their body and works. This is how a person shows or "bears fruit" in Jesus' blessed name. These two forms must be present within an individual for them to be justified and qualify to partake in the Lord's grace.

Without the *intellectual* part of faith (confessing/believing Jesus is the Son of God, and the gospel; repenting), there cannot be the inward; without the *inward* (Holy Spirit, faith *of* Jesus Christ) there cannot be justification before God. Therefore, the two *must* be simultaneously present in order for true faith to be found within an individual.

Justification in the original Greek is *dikaiosis* (dik-ah'-yo-sis) meaning, "Acquittal (for Christ's sake)." Quite wonderful it is to have this word applied to us (the saints) while standing before God the Father. It is only by Christ's love that this happens. A more layman meaning is used for those not so familiar with the term: Justification is "just as you never did it;" In this case, never sinned and violated the will of God.

The *inward* part of faith is Christ; the *intellectual* part is the faith of man. It is the *inward* part in which calls a man; it is the *intellectual* part in which the man accepts the call. It is the *inward* part in which convicts a man of His sin; it is the *intellectual* part in which the man willingly trusts in God to help and lead him to repentance. Remember, Paul says *we* are to put off the old man and put on the new (Colossians 3:9,10). So be not fooled when people say that Jesus took up *your* cross, for Jesus says that we are to take up our own cross, or else, we are not worthy of Him (Matthew 10:38).

I believe this to be a beautiful thing in accordance to the faith. Do you remember when God said in Isaiah 1:18, "Come now, and let us reason together..." That word "reason" there is from the original Hebrew word *yakach* (yaw-kahh') meaning, "to be right (i.e. correct); to decide, justify or convict." The Father will not force a man to be His child. At the appropriate time, God will call upon the man and give him the opportunity to become His child. He will allow the man to decide, or play a part, in whether or not he wishes to serve the everlasting King.

For all of you who are saying that it is by *our* faith alone in Jesus that we are justified, might I remind you what the apostle states in Galatians 2:16, "Knowing that a man is not justified by the works of the law, but by the faith of Jesus Christ, even we have believed in Jesus Christ, that we might be justified by the faith of Christ..." Catch that? We believe *in* Him (intellectual) but it is the faith *of* Him (inward; Holy Spirit) that justifies us before the Father. A sinful man cannot be a mediator for himself when he stands before God and expect to enter heaven. It is only by having the Son as your Mediator and Advocate will one be allowed in (1 John 2:1,2).

His faith (as stated in Galatians 2:20) is what we begin to walk in once we are crucified and dead to the world. It is He walking *through* us as we abide *in* Him. Revelation 2:13, Jesus says, "...and thou holdest fast my name, and hast not denied my faith..." This is only further confirmation of it being *His* faith and *His* works done in *His* name upon our rebirth and during the progression of our growing faith *in* Him.

One quick note to add to this: In order for us to have His faith, it must be Him living inside of us. This is the Holy Spirit. So Christ must be present within us for His faith to gain us God's grace. This is how the

Father (who is Spirit) sees His Son instead of us upon appearing before Him after death. It's very beautiful!

There are levels of faith: There are some with only a little faith - this is what one could gather a person begins with in which God imparts upon them. Those whom fail in growing such faith are shaky in their belief and in dangerous territory concerning their eternal future.

One of the most well known Baptist pastors in America once said "The strength of one's faith matters not." I believe that you can have very little faith and still go to heaven if you abide in Him and do His will despite your weak faith. But it, most of the time, requires much faith in order to continue in His will as a man will grow in the faith. A man need only to read the parable of the sower in Luke 8 to find out that those whom believe (have faith), if it be not strong enough to abide in Him, they fall away. Weak faith is dangerous, my friend.

There are those with average and the most commonly seen faith. These are those whom require more study and growth before reaching a level of comfortable intimacy with God. They have potential and may desire to come into a closer relationship with God, but are usually distracted by worldly things, family and/or relationships issues and have not the headstrong will required to come into perfection. These are the ones, who know little about the Bible, nor do they ever read the Word and when they do they find it too difficult to grasp.

Then, there are those rare few with great faith - they are the disciples, martyrs and risk-takers for Christ. Those whose prayers are the sweet incense in His tabernacle. They are infatuated with the knowledge of God, constantly hungry and ready to receive the most in-depth relationship that can possibly be obtained with God through Jesus Christ. Whether poor or rich, in whatever circumstance, Christ is King to these whom abide in faith.

My hope in this chapter is to show that faith is an ongoing characteristic of the Christian life, not temporary and something left behind or ignored. Faith is what is required before the Holy Spirit can indwell within a man. The Holy Spirit then aides the individual in keeping their faith, along with walking in God's will, and, ultimately, attaining the prize of eternal life in the end.

The great faith chapter of Hebrews 11 is a fantastic starting point for this. We will try to show how a promise was made by the Lord to an individual; the individual then had faith that the promise would be kept; as years went by, their faith allowed them to stay the course of God's will until, finally, the promise was fulfilled.

So let's begin: We will start out with Hebrews 11:7, "By faith Noah, being warned of God of things not seen as yet, moved with fear, prepared an ark to the saving of his house; by the which he condemned the world, and became heir of the righteousness which is by faith." Many refer to Noah's ark as a type of Christ; I believe this to be true. The flood was God's wrath upon the world for their wickedness and Noah was saved from God's wrath due to his faith. But let's examine this a bit closer.

Noah was given a promise by the Lord that He would destroy all flesh with the earth (Genesis 6:13), but he would save Noah, his family, and preserve a small remnant of each kind of beast with an ark. Noah was told what he should do (was given God's will and commandment) and did just as he was told. He could have easily have not done anything at all after God commanded him, but he chose to have faith and do what the Lord said. He was then saved on the day of wrath.

God's wrath is what awaits all unrepentant sinners upon death. To truly believe in Jesus is to believe every word He says. When He says to not lay up treasures on this earth but in heaven, you do that. When He says except you repent, you will likewise perish, you believe that. This is to truly believe in Christ. To take the Word at His word. To repent is to turn one's back on the worldly pleasures because, like Jesus said, you believe a greater life waits with Him. This is truly believing and having faith in Him. Repentance is felt inwardly and will show outwardly. To repent is to have *the* faith.

To believe that Jesus Christ is the Son of God is to take Him at His word. To do this is to believe Christ, which is to believe *in* Christ. When Jesus says there are many mansions in heaven, I believe what He says. When Jesus says before there was Abraham, He was, I believe Him. In the same manner, we should also believe Him when He says that if we love Him, we should obey His commandments. The unrepentant man does not do this therefore He does not love Him. And he whom does not love Him will not enter into the kingdom. For love is the fulfillment of the law (Romans 13:8-10, James 2:8) and those whom do not love God are under the law and cursed.

Faith is a few things: It is believing that which has been told to you without seeing, or, in other words, hope; it is that foundational connection which binds the man to the Lord; it is the root and beginning point of all works which are from and for God. We whom are the faithful know that God never lies, and are therefore well aware that we should always do His will and not our own. Not doing so is backsliding, this is the reason why all backsliders are called to repent and come back into the will of God before it's too late; only wrath awaits them (Hebrews 10:26,27).

Hebrews 11:8-10 speaks of Abraham, "By faith Abraham, when he was called to go out into a place which he should after receive for an inheritance, obeyed; and he went out, not knowing whither he went. By faith he sojourned in the land of promise, as in a strange country, dwelling in tabernacles with Isaac and Jacob, the heirs with him of the same promise: For he looked for a city which hath foundations, whose builder and maker is God."

There are many examples of Abraham's faith in which to state. One of which is he being called by the Lord God to leave his homeland solely reliant upon God's promise to lead him somewhere else. He had no clue as to where he was even going! He was first given the promise, then, by faith, left his homeland. After many trials along the way, he kept the faith, and arrived in the land of Canaan, which would later be known as Israel.

Because Abraham believed God it was counted unto him as righteousness (Romans 4:3). But because he truly believed and had faith in God, he did as God commanded him. As a result of Abraham having within him the faith he remained faithful in doing what God commanded him. Do you see how keeping God's commandments and being obedient to the faith are a clear showing and natural by-product of one possessing the true faith?

Verse 11 goes on, "Through faith also Sara herself received strength to conceive seed, and was delivered of a child when she was past age, because she judged him faithful who had promised." Abraham's wife Sara was well past the age of childbearing but she was given a promise from God that she would bear Abraham's child. She had faith that He was faithful in His promise to her. She continued in the faith and, in the end, Isaac was born, the promise was given.

Do you see how patience is of necessity in faith? Faith is not momentary, but something stretched out and tested time and time again. For all whom have faith, they know to walk in obedience to God's will in order so that the promise of eternal life is given in the end. Jesus gave us a promise of eternal life with Him, we must live in the faith of Him so that the Father will fulfill that promise until the prize is given, which comes at the end of our faithful lives.

Luke 12:42-48 is a great parable to illustrate this. Jesus speaks of a servant of the lord of the house being given a promise to all that the lord has if the servant remains faithful and wise until his coming. But if the lord returns to his house and finds the servant being disobedient, wicked, and drunken, the lord will "cut him in sunder, and will appoint him his portion with the unbelievers."

Notice what Jesus says in His parable of the talents in Matthew 25:14-30; He likens the kingdom of heaven to a master entrusting a certain amount of money to his three servants. Two of them go out and double their investment (or bear fruit); the other, for fear of his master, buries his talent and returns it to him upon his return. The two which profited for the master are rewarded for their faithfulness/obedience; the other, which was called "wicked and slothful" or self-serving and lazy, was cast "into outer darkness."

What the master says to the faithful servants in verses 21 and 23 is important, "Well done, thou good and faithful servant: thou hast been faithful over a few things, I will make thee ruler over many things: enter thou into the joy of thy lord."

I would like to take this time to put to rest any of the reader's beliefs that may cling to the thought of faith only consisting of momentary belief in Christ and nothing else. After the many instances in which I have shown you already how faith will breed works in Christ's name, I believe that no one could argue with the verses of James 2:14-18:

"What doth it profit, my brethren, though a man say he hath faith, and have not works? can faith save him? If a brother or sister be naked, and destitute of daily food, and one of you say unto them, Depart in peace, be ye warmed and filled; notwithstanding ye give them not those things which are needful to the body; what doth it profit? Even so faith, if it hath not works, is dead, being alone. Yea, a man may say, Thou hast faith, and I have works: shew me thy faith without thy works, and I will shew thee my faith by my works..."

This is what Jesus meant in His conclusion of the sower parable in Luke 8:15, "But [the seed] on the good ground are they; which in an honest and good heart, having heard the word, keep it, and bring forth fruit with patience." If a man has faith, he will bear fruit.

Faith is also tested throughout the believer's walk in Christ. 1 Peter 1:7 says to believers, "That the trial of your faith, being much more precious than of gold that perisheth, though it be tried with fire, might be found unto praise and honour and glory at the appearing of Jesus Christ..." Our foundation is faith and it is tested through trials and temptations of the flesh to see if one chooses God's will over their own.

Notice how the verse ends with "might be found unto praise and honour and glory," speaking of our faith. Such glowing attributes can only be seen in the overcoming of earthly pleasures. One must ask then, what happens to those whose faith is not found unto praise and honor and glory?

Colossians 1:21-23 states, "And you, that were sometime alienated and enemies in your mind by wicked works, yet now hath he reconciled in the body of his flesh through death, to present you holy and unblameable and unreproveable in his sight: if ye continue in the faith grounded and settled, and be not moved away from the hope of the gospel, which ye have heard..." One could derive from verse 23 that if one does not remain grounded and continue in the faith, and is moved away, that they will not be reconciled to the Father.

Jude 20, 21 states, "But ye, beloved, building up yourselves on your most holy faith, praying in the Holy Ghost, keep yourselves in the love of God, looking for the mercy of our Lord Jesus Christ unto eternal life."

This is obviously saying that we are to pray in our most holy faith (with the Holy Spirit) to build up ourselves, in order so that we are strengthened in Jesus Christ. Verse 21 goes on to emphasize how we are to *keep ourselves* in the love of God (implying an act of abiding in the faith that we do not fall out of His love and allow our hearts to be hardened to His glory again), in which we can look for the mercy of our Lord Jesus Christ unto eternal life.

When the two thieves were hanging on both sides of Jesus at the cross, notice how He never begged either of them to believe in Him. He waited for them to make the decision for themselves as to what they believed. One rejected Him; the other believed in Him. One entered into eternal torment; the other into paradise. My point in this is the faith of that one whom believed in Him. Faith gives willingness and a yearning to admit our guilt, come to Christ and do His will, even to the point of death.

Many professing Christians only claim belief in Christ because they don't want to go to hell, but true Christians will be as the thief in which truly believed in Him as the Son of God. One mocked Christ because he seen that He wasn't going to help him break free from his punishment (he only looked at himself and his own situation) like those whom call upon Him to relieve them of hell; the other seen his own guilt, his certainty of deserving the punishment, and the innocence of Christ Jesus, he then asked only that Christ remember him in the afterlife. Faith is a reliance upon Christ and not self. It is about allowing self to die and Christ to be your life.

Faith is a spiritual thing, an ongoing belief, not a mere thought. It is something in which must be exercised in the heart of a man. The book of Acts 6:7 states, "...a great company of the priests were *obedient* to the faith." The faith is a thing in which carries with it moral content. It demands obedience. It changes lives. It makes dirty people clean; wicked people holy; lazy people active; and dead people alive.

Romans 1:5, Paul writes, "For whom we have recieved grace and apostleship, for *obedience* to the faith among all nations, for his name:" and in Romans 16:26, "But now is made manifest... to all nations for the *obedience* of faith." So faith in Christ demands obedience. Argue all you like but obedience is clearly an important attribute of faith to God.

Jesus said to the afflicted woman in Mark 5:34, "Daughter, thy faith hath made thee whole..." All this woman had done was believed and touched His garment; His virtue healed her, but Jesus said Himself that it was her *faith* that triggered His virtue. But notice what else happened, verse 33 states that the woman fell down before Him, fearing and trembling, and told Him all the truth. That very same faith brought with it fear and trembling, as well as public profession.

With fear of the Lord comes willing obedience and reverential awe. Those whom call Christ "Lord" and truly mean and believe it will fear Him, as well as the Father, and, as a result, be obedient. Those whom call Him "Lord" and only profess it will find themselves ignorantly not fearing the Lord, nor giving reverence to Him, and as a result, they are disobedient. Point being - the disobedient have not the true faith.

The thief on the cross' obedient walk of faith began immediately after he believed in Christ. He first truly believed (had faith and became a willing servant) in Him, and then acknowledged his own guilt and Christ's innocence upon the cross. The thief was at that moment justified due to his faith before his death. The difference between his obedient walk and ours is his began in the afterlife. He now walks in

God's will constantly, just as we are all expected to do if we are dead to the world and Christ lives and works within us.

One act of faith being shown in great illustration of both the consequence of lacking it and the beauty of repentance is shown in Matthew 14:29-31, "...And when Peter was come down out of the ship, he walked on the water, to go to Jesus. But when he saw the wind boisterous, he was afraid; and beginning to sink, he cried, saying, Lord, save me. And immediately Jesus stretched forth his hand, and caught him, and said unto him, O thou of little faith, wherefore didst thou doubt?"

I have heard this event used by defenders of O.S.A.S. preachers to prove that even though Peter took his eyes of Jesus and began to sink, Jesus still reached out and caught him. But, notice the three words in which Peter yelled out *before* Jesus reached out and helped him - "Lord, save me." This is a clear showing of repentance for those in whom take their eyes off of Christ. Only when Peter yelled out for Christ did Jesus help him out of the water. Let this also be a showing that God will not fill a vessel which is already full by itself; He will work through only those who are emptied (Matthew 9:17). This will bear much fruit as it will then be Christ Jesus working through you instead of yourself. Your will becomes His will and you are truly one with Him.

When Jesus turned the water into wine in John 2, before He did so, He commanded the servants to fill the water pots. He then made the wine. Before Jesus raised Lazarus from the dead in John 11, He ordered the people to take away the stone. He then resurrected Lazarus. My point is that there are things required of us before the promise is fulfilled.

Another example of our faithful actions being a natural overflow of the faith is found when Jesus says in Matthew 6:14,15, "For if ye forgive men their trespasses, your heavenly Father will also forgive you: But if ye forgive not men their trespasses, neither will your Father forgive your trespasses."

Also in Matthew 18:23-35, we read of how the kingdom of heaven is likened to a certain king forgiving a servant of his massive debt, only to find out afterwards that that same servant failed in forgiving a fellow servant of his small debt. Upon hearing this, the king is overcome with wrath and delivers the servant to the tormentors. Jesus concluded the parable in verse 35, "So likewise shall my heavenly Father do also unto you, if ye from your hearts forgive not every one his brother their trespasses."

So it is this faithful work of forgiveness in which contributes to the Lord's mercy on us. Not a simple reliance on God's part to overlook us when we treat men the same as before our rebirth. A Christ-like quality in which is found only in true saints of

God further extending our knowledge of what accompanies *the* faith.

Faith also brings forth unabashed confession. Jesus Christ said in Luke 9:46, "For whosoever shall be ashamed of me and of my words, of him shall the Son of man be ashamed, when he shall come in his own glory, and in his Father's, and of the holy angels." Once again, this is a showing and/or work of faith, not merely believing, which carries with it repercussions if not enacted. Let no man deceive you into thinking that works mean nothing in accordance to faith. Godly works is a showing of faith. It is the fruit we bear. It shows the man's heart, whether it be of Christ or of himself. The unrepentant will usually remain in ignorance because someone has told them that any works we do means nothing. Blood will be on the hands of such who say these things.

I have heard believers cite 2 Timothy 2:13 where it says, "If we believe not, yet he abideth faithful: he cannot deny himself." Some quote this in reference to a man still being within God's good grace because He is faithful even though the once-believer is found faithless. That is *not* what this verse is saying at all. Begin by reading verses 11 and 12 beforehand, this will put the verse in its proper context.

Paul says, "It is a faithful saying: For if we be dead with him, we shall also live with him: If we suffer, we shall also reign with him: if we deny him, he also will deny us." Remember Paul said he had to "die daily," so every day is a dying experience to self, not a one time event where afterwards we can live like the devil. "If we suffer" is a matter of enduring, not a mere moment of pain followed by worldly indulgence. And finally, "if we deny him, he also will deny us" is a statement in which places verse 13 in its proper context.

It is therefore safe to conclude that verse 13 is speaking to those in whom either is found to be faithless entirely (atheists), or who once were faithful and have, after a time, fallen from the faith. By stating that God is faithful is a way of saying that God is immutable. All of the rules and judgments He has set in place will not be brushed aside in order to give us license to do what we want. If we remain with Him, He is faithful in keeping us; if we fall from Him in our hearts, He is faithful in letting us go.

Worth citing in relation to these verses is Titus 1:16, "They profess that they know God; but in works they deny him, being abominable, and disobedient, and unto every good work reprobate." For those of you who believe works count for nothing after you are reborn, this clearly says that works show our denial of God and remember what Paul says in 2 Timothy 2:12, "...if we deny him, he also will deny us:"

Let us also not forget 1 Corinthians 4:2, "Moreover it is required in stewards, that a man be found faithful." Notice the Holy Spirit states "required" not suggested that a man be found faithful.

Remember this: The very same person that you are now; whether you hate sin and all the pleasures of this world, or love it, is the very same *you* in which will be in eternity. The flesh carries with it temptations and afflictions, these are the means (for the most part) in which one can be tried (tested) by "fire" (read the book of Job for proof of this). But it is the real you in whom either chooses to reject those temptations and do God's will or fall into them.

My point in saying this is that there will be no rebels in heaven, no disobedience. If you live your days on this earth doing what you want to do instead of God's sovereign will, I don't care how many sinner's prayers you've said, you will not be in God's home. Your true self will show while you live here.

I often liken it to a stranger knocking on your door and asking if he can live the rest of his life with you and your family. He doesn't ever plan on obeying your rules, following your ways, being there when you need him. The only thing that he plans on doing is using up as much of your resources as he can so that he may do all the things that he wishes to do. Any logical person would never allow such a person into his home. What makes you think God will be any different?

Faith breeds love, true love, for God. I once argued with a person whom was contending for the popularized O.S.A.S. doctrine, she said to me, "God is love, He is not up there judging our every move. He is love above ALL other things." But love is something in which demands many things. It demands obedience, trust, loyalty, acceptance, etc. It is something in which establishes a greater spiritual and emotional connection to that which it is attached to.

Love is also a natural affection that accompanies faith. I have done many things in which I had no desire to do, yet still did, simply out of love. My mother may have asked me to clean my room, I did not want to, but none-the-less, and I did, because I love her. She had faith in me that I would clean the room; I had faith that she would be appeased by me cleaning the room; the order was therefore obeyed due to a real mutual faith in between us two. I was faithful in my promise to her; she was faithful in not arguing with me since the order was obeyed; Peace resided between us.

God is the same with us. Those with true faith may not wish to do many things in which the Father may ask of us. It is due to us having faith (love, trust, willing obedience, etc.) and loving Him that we do His will regardless of our own feelings towards it. A man may claim to have this faith, but by his laziness and unwillingness to do that which God ask of him, he shows that he has not true faith, and, therefore, is not in His grace. He does not "bear fruit."

Many have I met in which believe that the only requirement of heaven is that they be nice and polite in order to wind up there after this life. It's not about being nice and polite, though. There are many very cordial atheists whom have no desire whatsoever to do God's will.

The Lord's will is not about being simply nice, as so many who do not know him believe so fervently. Many times, His will was to send a famine on the land. He ordered that whole armies and nations should be wiped out. It was not very nice when Jesus made a whip and began lashing the moneychangers in the temple, was it? His will is sovereign and one must have true faith in order to do it.

This is why Jesus said in Matthew 7:16-20 that you will know a person, be they of God or evil, by their fruits. He did not say by a prayer that they say one night, or by their religious background or appearance, but by their fruits (works of obedience to God's will in Jesus' name).

I believe that simply believing (having faith) in Jesus' name is all that is required to attain salvation - I truly do. But further elaboration is required in order to better understand such a statement, as many gather a far too simple, and altogether, damning meaning from the words when taken by themselves.

If you believe that Jesus is the Son of God, then you believe that He is the King of kings and Lord of lords. This is an incredibly exalted position to place anyone in and He is the only Man worthy of taking such a position. But *belief* is a tricky word; it is either thinking something to be true or knowing it on the inside. To *think* something and truly *believe* it are two different things.

Let me illustrate: I can think that the ocean is very deep and the sky is very high, indeed, most of us think this and believe it to be true. But, I only begin to fully believe and respect such a reality (it sinks in) when I am swimming deep in a dark part of a lake or climbing a tree to hunt from and suddenly look down. It is the fear of the reality; the all-encompassing nature of being engulfed in its majesty that fully brings my belief full swing into being real and truly present within me.

Where before I had a very shallow concept of the ocean being deep and the sky being high, I now *truly* believe it in the awful sense of the word. My belief in it is now real and not superficial. Though it was only a mere fraction of the water's depth and the sky's height, I can now never be convinced of any other reality being true because I have experienced for myself that the waters of earth are deep and the sky is high.

Belief in Jesus is the same way. Many only *think* that He is the Son of God. This is good, but that faith often left to itself becomes dry and weak. Having stagnant faith was, I believe, what caused me to fall from grace all those years ago. It is when you truly yearn to come into the knowing presence of His majesty that His virtue begins to manifest itself in your deepest being in which only God Himself has access to.

A man cannot claim to have such a knowledge of God (a *true* belief in Him, which the Holy Spirit is the Strengthener of such things) without the fear and reverential awe which accompanies it being present within him as well; Without the prayers of anguish and the guilt of hurting Him when you sin against Him; Without the willingness to do His will and spread the glorious message of His Son Jesus Christ. This is the true belief - the true faith!

It is this true faith in which changes a man from a child of Adam to a child of the King. It is also this faith in which some can (and do) leave even after experiencing it for themselves. Jesus spoke of such a thing in Matthew 13.

So let us not mistake having faith in Jesus Christ to be a simple thing in which (like the ocean's depth, or the sky's height) we have only heard about, or watched in movies, or read in books. It is a good saying: "Many know the word of God, but few know the God of the word."

Faith is something in which carries with it a personal connection, friendship, and a willing servitude to God and His glorious Son. It is an ongoing, life-changing, and wonderful experience, not a simple belief (in the ordinary sense of the word) that is to imply a mere thought or acknowledgment of Jesus being God's Son. Many have I seen do this simply because they were afraid of dying and going to hell.

The best parable to illustrate the importance of God seeing action as more important than mere profession can be found in Matthew 21:28-30). It says, "...a certain man had two sons; and he came to the first, and said, Son, go work to day in my vineyard. He answered and said, I will not: but afterward he repented and went. And he came to the second, and said likewise. And he answered and said, I go, sir: and went not. Whether of them twain did the will of his father? They say unto him, The first..."

Like James 1:22 states, "But be ye doers of the word, and not hearers only, deceiving your own selves." The faith is something in which action will be taken due to its impact on a person's life.

The faith must be understood for what it is - a living thing that can be found great and steadfast, or dead. If it were dead, then it is no longer valid. If it were dead, then the individual is found without the faith that is the only thing that can place one under His grace.

Mere profession is one thing which most have always done. Matthew 15:8, Jesus quoted Isaiah saying, "This people draweth nigh unto me with their mouth, and honoureth me with their lips; but their heart is far from me." Be sure to have the required oil for your lamp on that great day. Make certain you have the faith *of* Jesus Christ as well as the faith *in* Jesus Christ, the Amen and the good Friend!

CHAPTER 10

THE SHEEP AND GOATS

Great and mighty King, I beseech Thee to impart knowledge within Your humble and forever thankful servant in order so that he might do Thy will, O Lord. Grant unto me the continued wisdom of Thee to only speak truth, and that You may bless these readers. Blessed be the Lamb and Lion of Judah!!! Blessed be Thy name above heaven and earth! Amen

Let us now refer back to what Jesus says of the sheep and the goats in Matthew 25. Jesus is speaking here of the characteristics one will have if they are His disciples. The sheep are the ones entering into heaven and the Lord is telling them why. We will first focus on them:

Verse 34 begins, "Then shall the King say unto them on his right hand, Come, ye blessed of my

Father, inherit the kingdom prepared for you from the foundation of the world: For I was hungered, and ye gave me meat: I was thirsty, and ye gave me drink: I was a stranger, and ye took me in: Naked, and ye clothed me: I was sick, and ye visited me: I was in prison, and ye came unto me. Then shall the righteous answer him, saying, Lord, when saw we thee an hungred, and fed thee? or thirsty, and gave thee drink? When saw we thee a stranger, and took thee in? or naked, and clothed thee? Or when saw we thee sick, or in prison, and came unto thee? And the King shall answer and say unto them, Verily I say unto you, Inasmuch as ye have done it unto one of the least of these my brethren, ye have done it unto me."

His children are expected to always do justly to all men. James, whom wrote the epistle of James in the New Testament, was called James the Just. He was one of the half-brothers of Jesus Christ while on earth. He was known for being so devout and pious that his knees were calloused over by the time he died because he prayed so often and for so long. He wrote his epistle to remind people of the importance of living out their faith, not merely proclaiming it.

He wrote in James 1:27, "Pure religion and undefiled before God and the Father is this, To visit the fatherless and widows in their affliction, and to keep himself unspotted from the world."

This was also important for the believers in God before Christ came, Micah 6:6-8, "Wherewith shall I come before the LORD and bow myself before the high God? shall I come before him with burnt offerings, with calves of a year old? Will the LORD be pleased with thousands of rams, or with ten thousands of rivers of oil? shall I give my firstborn for my transgression, the fruit of my body for the sin of my soul? He hath shewed thee, O man, what is good; and what doth the LORD require of thee, but to do justly, and to love mercy, and to walk humbly with thy God?"

We have become lax and comfortable in *once saved, always saved.* The world is suffering and more in need of Christ than ever, yet we sit back and apathetically bathe in grace. But know you not that the devil can give comfort as well as God? He gives it to many! The realm of hell is filled with people who were comfortable all their lives before falling into hades utterly shocked.

It says in 1 Peter 4:12-14, "Beloved, think it not strange concerning the fiery trial which is to try you, as though some strange thing happened unto you: But rejoice, inasmuch as ye are partakers of Christ's sufferings; that, when his glory shall be revealed, ye may be glad also with exceeding joy. If ye be reproached for the name of Christ, happy are ye; for this the spirit of glory and of God resteth upon you:

on their part he is evil spoken of, but on your part he is glorified."

John 15:20, Jesus says, "...if they persecuted me, they will also persecute you..." The Church has never been so conformed to the world than it is now. The most famous pastors are being invited to the White House; was Elijah ever invited to Ahab's palace? Was John invited to Herod's palace? Was Paul invited to Caesar's? Only when the kings wished to cut their heads off were they brought before them!

Supposedly, most Americans are "saved." What a wretched thing! One could not even tell that there are Christians in America if it wasn't for the church houses and crosses everywhere. We love to say we are Christians, but not live it. We love to carry with us the lamps but forget the oil. Christians used to be dirty on the outside and clean on the inside; Now they are clean on the outside and dirty inside.

Too many "Christians" have no fear of God within them anymore. One famous celebrity (which I will not name) once said, "For me, there doesn't need to be a God." Many Christians share this sentiment, only they are unaware that they have no God either. They have something in which they call God. They may show up for church, tithe, watch religious shows and speak of God on a regular basis, but one cannot distinguish them from the rest of the world. God is a *get-out-of-hell* free card for them.

The Pharisees were the most religious of all the people in Israel. They did everything in which they should do, but like the virgins Jesus spoke of in Matthew 25, they had no oil to light their lamps once the bridegroom arrived. The oil is that of the true faith on the inside, which shows outwardly through the light.

I speak not only to the outright sinners whom proclaim Christ as Lord of their lives but to the self-righteous as well. People who have a sort of higher-than-thou complex and tell others that unless they live like them they will not enter into heaven. These claim that God will only accept the sinless person, but it is the heart that God looks upon. They may dress their lamps up and carry them everywhere they go. Even in secret, they may covet their lamp and think highly of it. But what is a lamp without oil? What is a lamp without light? Nothing. Only a dead decoration that will perish in the darkness like the holder of it.

Jesus used another illustration of these "dead" Christians without true faith when he spoke of the Pharisees being as whited sepulchres (Matthew 23:27). He said they "indeed appear beautiful outward, but are within full of dead men's bones, and of all uncleanness."

Jesus said in John 8:12, "...I am the light of the world: he that followeth me shall not walk in darkness, but shall have the light of life." He also states in

Matthew 5:14,15, "Ye are the light of the world. A city that is set on an hill cannot be hid. Neither do men light a candle, and put it under a bushel, but on a candlestick; and it giveth light unto all that are in the house." A light reveals what the darkness hides, therefore those who walk in darkness have no light. One can only gather that if an individual proclaiming to be a Christian walks in darkness like the world (and you can tell if they are by their fruit), then they have not the light of life and do not follow Jesus.

They whom have secrets in which they hide from the world and believe themselves to hide from God are not of God. Jesus says in John 18:20, "...in secret have I said nothing." Nothing is hidden where light resides, therefore if one has light he has no secrets or hidden things. I fear for so many of my Freemason friends out there.

I have heard many argue that there will be no judgment for the Christians upon death. No accountability is required for the reborn, they say. But what does Paul say in Romans 14:10, "...for we shall all stand before the judgment seat of Christ." He goes on in verse 12, "...then every one of us shall give account of himself to God."

It is this kind of thinking which hinders the fear of God within a person. Such a belief also pervades every corner of the *once saved, always saved* believers of today. Once the fear of God is gone, so is wisdom, only apathy remains. Once again, Hosea 4:6 is a stunning reality among the people after that.

My good Pastor friend once told the story of a fellow Pastor's wife having a flat tire on the side of the road on her way to church. All of the church members passed her by on their way to the church in which her husband was the Pastor of. An old man who never went to church had to come by and change her tire for her so that she could go to church. This is the type of character spoken of the hypocrites in which Christ refers to as the goats in Matthew 25:41-46:

"Then shall he say also unto them on the left hand, Depart from me, ye cursed, into everlasting fire, prepared for the devil and his angels: For I was an hungred, and ye gave me no meat: I was thirsty, and ye gave me no drink: I was a stranger, and ye took me not in: naked, and ye clothed me not: sick, and in prison, and ye visited me not. Then shall they answer him, saying, Lord, when saw we thee an hungred, or athirst, or a stranger, or naked, or sick, or in prison, and did not minister unto thee? Then shall he answer them, saying, Verily I say unto you, Inasmuch as ye did it not to one of these, ye did it not to me. And these shall go away into everlasting punishment: but the righteous into life eternal."

I am well aware of those who say this relates to Israel and the judgment of those whom stand with or against her during tribulation. I am not saying that this does not pertain to them in the immediate context (but of such I do question as it is written that ALL nations shall be gathered against Israel in that day, none will help her according to Zechariah 12:3 and 14:2) but this also describes those whom have the Holy Ghost dwelling within them and the works of Christ in which they do in His name - help the hungry, thirsty, stranger, naked, sick, imprisoned. All of these things did Christ do while on earth and are likewise commanded of His disciples.

Jesus tells in Luke 13:6-9 the parable of the barren fig tree, it begins with, "A certain man had a fig tree planted in his vineyard; and he came and sought fruit thereon, and found none." The man is God, the fig tree is Israel. "Then said he unto the dresser of his vineyard, Behold, these three years I come seeking fruit on this fig tree, and find none: cut it down; why cumbereth it the ground?"

The dresser is Christ; the owner of the vineyard (God) wants to cut it down because it has not brought forth fruit for some time. "And he answering said unto him, Lord, let it alone this year also, till I shall dig about it, and dung it: And if it bear fruit, well: and if not, then after that thou shalt cut it down." This shows the patience in which God deals with backsliders like Israel and carnal Christians.

The verses preceding this parable are on the importance of repentance. Israel, like the Gentile believers of today, is God's people and had a habit of backsliding. All backsliders cease to bear fruit, but His mercy is extended due to His love and kindness towards them. But in the end, the fate is the same for all whom draw back, fail to repent, and, ultimately, fall away from God's grace and will. This is the reason why repentance is so stressed by Jesus throughout His ministry on earth. He says many things similar to verses 3 and 5, "... except ye repent, ye shall all likewise perish."

We will now take a look at the parable of the sower spoken by Jesus in Luke 8, it begins, "A sower went out to sow his seed: and as he sowed, some fell by the way side; and it was trodden down, and the fowls of the air devoured it. And some fell upon a rock; and as soon as it was sprang up, it withered away, because it lacked moisture. And some fell among thorns; and the thorns sprang up with it, and choked it. And other fell on good ground, and sprang up, and bare fruit an hundredfold."

Jesus goes on to explain the parable, He begins in verse 11, "Now the parable is this: The seed is the word of God. Those by the way side are they that hear; then cometh the devil, and taketh away the word out of their hearts, lest they should believe and be saved. They on the rock are they, which, when they hear, receive the word with joy; and these have no root, which for a while believe, and in time of temptation fall away. And that which fell among the thorns are they, which, when they have heard, go forth, and are choked with cares and riches and pleasures of this life, and bring forth no fruit to perfection. But that on the good ground are they, which in an honest and good heart, having heard the word, keep it, and bring forth fruit with patience."

Those sown on the stony ground and amongst the thorns are those in which I would like to highlight. These are much like those whom carry with them the popularized Eternal Security doctrine. They hear the truth, receive it in the beginning, then, after the world gets to them, turn from God's will. The difference is that they are comfortable in falling back into the world due to some preacher telling them that they are saved from the moment they say the prayer. Nothing of abiding or continuing in the faith. An eternity of wrath made void in a moment then everything is back to the same as before for the wretch the next moment. This is dangerous and, time and time again, I have shown that it is unbiblical, but I will continue in my showing in order to expose the truth of the doctrine to all who hears.

One last point of this parable I would like to make: Jesus relates the seed which fell on the good ground to them which, upon hearing the word, keep it, and bring forth fruit with patience. Jesus is reiterating the same point consistently throughout His ministry. That those whom hear the truth - the Word of God and the gospel - should keep it (in their hearts), and bring forth fruit (outwardly show their faithfulness through works in Christ's name) with patience (implying an ongoing life of servitude and faith in Christ Jesus).

John 13:15, Christ says, "For I have given you an example, that ye should do as I have done to you." He's speaking of Him washing their feet, for it is the will of God for His children to serve others and be humbled at all times; no other type of vessel can the LORD God work through. As Christ did on earth, so will His disciples do after Him. He accomplished many things on earth, but one thing often overlooked by believers of the popularized O.S.A.S. crowd is the example He set by His daily walk and deeds.

Everybody wants to be *with* Christ, but very few wish to be *like* Christ. But those are the ones whom enter into the kingdom. We are called the Bride of Christ, not the Brides. We shall be of one body and of one accord. We shall all be like Him, like He wants us to be, and not like we want to be ourselves.

It is not sin in which causes God's children to fall from grace, but rejecting God in one's heart for the world. For God sees the heart of man. The sin is simply a showing of their heart's change, much like righteous works are a showing of their heart's love for God. Those not of His fold are damned for their rejection, whether it be an acknowledged thing or something done in ignorance.

Christ says to the self-deceived Pharisees in John 8:21, "I go my way, and ye shall seek me, and shall die in your sins: whither I go, ye cannot come." He is telling them that if they die unrepentant, they will not be with Him in heaven. The same thing is found throughout the New Testament - if you die in an unrighteous state that is not of God (in other words, unrepentant in heart and failing to fully believe in Christ), then you will not be with God after death.

Jesus consistently proclaimed boldly that He only did the will of the Father God. In verse 41, He says, "Ye do the deeds of your father." Like many Christians today, they replied, "We be not of fornication; we have one Father, even God." He then goes on in verse 44, "Ye are of your father the devil, and the lusts of your father ye will do." This is very telling and many miss a crucial point of this saying: They of whom are of the devil will do those things in which the devil does - sin, or rebel against God's will. Though they may claim to love Jesus Christ, follow His ways, and fear God, they ultimately do what they want to do in spite of what the Lord wills for them to do with little to no remorse or conviction.

He then states in verse 51, "Verily, verily, I say unto you, If a man keep my saying, he shall never see death." Further verification that *keeping* His saying (staying in the faith) is of necessity in accordance to salvation.

I know that anytime a man quotes Old Testament verses in relation to salvation for the Church it is immediately viewed as pointless. So my point in quoting Deuteronomy 23:14 is to show how God requires holiness - always has, always will. It is written, "For the LORD thy God walketh in the midst of thy camp, to deliver thee, and to give up thine enemies before thee; therefore shall thy camp be holy: that he see no unclean thing in thee, and turn away from thee." A clear statement of uncleanness turning God away from man.

The difference between the law of Moses and the new covenant of Christ Jesus is best stated in Romans 8:3,4, "For what the law could not do, in that it was weak through the flesh, God sending his own Son in the likeness of sinful flesh, and for sin, condemned sin in the flesh: That the righteousness of the law might be fulfilled in us, who walk not after the flesh, but after the Spirit."

The Law of Moses showed how bad man is; Grace shows us how good God is. But to those whom call upon the Lord God, the Holy Spirit is then sent in order to make one holy and fulfill the law by making it possible to be holy and wholly for God. The Spirit now gives us the ability to be what God would want of us - obedient.

Remember what king David said in Psalm 24, "Who shall ascend into the hill of the LORD? or who shall stand in his holy place? He that hath clean hands, and a pure heart; who hath not lifted up his soul unto vanity, nor sworn deceitfully. He shall receive the blessing from the LORD, and righteousness from the God of his salvation."

That is the type of person who God is seeking; not a cold-hearted man with dirty hands with which he prayed the sinner's prayer one night and afterwards lived like the devil.

In 2 Corinthians 6:14-16, Paul writes, "Be ye not unequally yoked together with unbelievers: for what fellowship hath righteousness with unrighteousness? and what communion hath light with darkness? And what concord hath Christ with Belial? or what part hath he that believeth with an infidel? And what agreement hath the temple of God with idols? for ye are the temple of the living God; as God hath said, I will dwell in them, and walk in them; and I will be their God, and they shall be my people."

My point in this is the same as the sheep being separate from the goats. Notice how the writer relates the believers with righteousness and unbelievers with unrighteousness. This is a showing of a believer's character, which is righteousness through Christ Jesus in whom he follows; the unbelievers are characterized by their unrighteousness. He is judging them by their "fruit." How can the living, holy, and beautiful God reside inside of you if you are filled with worldly death, dirt, and ugliness? Simple answer: He cannot.

King David wrote in Psalm 34:14-16, "Depart from evil, and do good; seek peace, and pursue it. The eyes of the LORD are upon the righteous, and his ears are open unto their cry. The face of the LORD is against them that do evil, to cut off the remembrance of them from the earth." The sheep bare good fruit; the goats - evil. The LORD God loves only those who are found to be righteous through His Son and despises those who do evil and have it in their hearts. If He felt this way then, nothing has changed (Hebrews 13:8).

Let us now examine what Paul wrote in Romans 11:16-22; it says, "...if the root be holy, so are the branches. And if some of the branches be broken off, and thou, being a wild olive tree, wert graffed in among them, and with them partakers of the root and fatness of the olive tree; Thou wilt say then, The branches were broken off, that I might be graffed in. Well; because of unbelief they were broken off, and thou standest by faith. Be not highminded, but fear: For if God spared not the natural branches, take heed lest he also spare not thee. Behold therefore the goodness and severity of God: on them which fell, severity; but toward thee, goodness, if thou continue in his goodness: otherwise thou also shalt be cut off."

Paul is speaking here of Israel being the natural branches which were cut off and the Church being the branches which were grafted in. He states in verse 20 that some Israelites were broken off due to their unbelief (a testament to a lack of faith resulting in falling from grace - 2 Timothy 2:11-13). He also mentions that the Church stands on faith in the root (which is Christ). He goes on to state that in verse 22 His goodness is towards the Church only if we continue in His goodness, otherwise we will be as some of the Israelites - cut off.

This clearly illustrates how we must continue in faith and not merely give a temporary show of it. Like the dividing of the sheep and the goats, God will separate those who are doers of His will from those who are only sayers and/or are disobedient to it, the likes of which is damnation.

CHAPTER 11

SALVATION

Blessed art Thou O Most High God! In Whom I trust and love with all of my life, I thank Thou most merciful Lamb for giving all unto us, whom are less than nothing. You have given us grace, and the Lion of Judah is most glorious and gracious in His kindness! May He be lifted along with Thee exalted O Most High LORD God. Walk with me, Amen

The free gift of eternal life from God is the most priceless gift in which a man could ever receive. So precious few receive it, but blessed are they whom do. We will now endeavor to speak on when this most glorious gift is imparted unto a believer. This I shall do, with God's help, in the most thorough way as possible. This is when we are truly saved, I believe.

We have all transgressed the laws of God (Romans 3:23). Man was created holy and could share in fellowship with God in the beginning. After man fell, we were stripped of the most intimate relationship we can have, which is with our Creator - God.

Romans 6:23 says, "For the wages of sin is death: but the gift of God is eternal life through Jesus Christ our Lord." It is the all-important gift. I will not in any way dispute that. I truly believe that it is a free gift and one that cannot be worked for. No merit of ours holds any weight in accordance with our everlasting salvation.

Paul writes in Romans 3:27, "Where is boasting then? It is excluded. By what law? of works? Nay: but by the law of faith." I have not once listed, nor found in any of my studies of the Holy Bible, where it says that works pertain in gaining grace from God. The entire point of this book is to clear up the slight confusion of true salvation, which is the free gift of eternal life from God.

Though we should emphasize where the importance of works comes into play. The works in which we do before being granted grace are *our* works (filthy and worthless); the works in which we do after being granted grace are God's works (which is the bearing of good fruit). I believe these works are two things: a showing of the faith by the bearing of good fruit; and the manner in which we may attain rewards in the next life.

In order to add a bit of clarity to this I will quote Paul from Philippians 2:12,13, "Wherefore, my beloved, as ye have always obeyed, not as in my presence only, but now much more in my absence, work out your own salvation with fear and trembling. For it is God which worketh in you both to will and to do of his good pleasure."

This is not to be confused with believing that we can save ourselves through works, but that God is individually saving us because we are humbled through fear and trembling before Him, and are thereby allowing Him to work in and through us. If the popularized O.S.A.S. is true, what need is there of "fear and trembling?" No matter what an individual who believes in such a doctrine does after they say the sinner's prayer, they believe they are going to heaven.

I have heard it claimed by certain believers in the popularized O.S.A.S. that God will "take them out of the world" if they fall too far from Him. It seems to me not to be such a dire punishment - do anything I want on this earth after my rebirth, if God "takes me out" then I get to go to heaven for eternity, if not, I will continue in doing whatever I please as my salvation is secure.

Not only is this belief illogical, it is dangerous to one's soul. Though I have heard many preachers of Eternal Security discourage their flocks against living a sinful lifestyle after an individual is reborn, they never tell of the ultimate consequence of falling in such a way. I believe even a few of them notice an inconsistency in the doctrine and thereby remain willingly silent when preaching it.

I have witnessed even very well known pastors steer away from the subject of what occurs when a truly reborn individual falls from God. They seem to be extremely cautious in only focusing on the dangers of backsliding and not stating the ultimate consequence of it.

When Jesus declares and opens His ministry with the words that have since forever changed the history of all the world for all time (Matthew 4:17), "Repent: for the kingdom of heaven is at hand." He said something often overlooked by people. That word "repent" in the original writing of Greek is *metanoeo* (met-an-o-eh'-o) meaning "to think differently" implying turn away from your transgressions against the Lord; it does NOT mean to think differently at that moment then go back to the way you were thinking; it doesn't mean to pray at the altar then go back and live like the world.

Other Greek words used in the original writings are *metamellomai* (met-am-el'-lom-ahee), meaning to "regret" and *metanoia* (met-an'-oy-ah) meaning "compunction (for guilt, including reformation); by implication - reversal." So, the three words used in the original writings for *repent* mean to regret, feel guilt, think differently, reform, reverse your ways; in essence - to change.

If all that is required of heaven is to only believe on Christ (in the sense of proclaiming to love Him and always say that He is the Son of God), then why did Jesus begin His ministry on earth by telling every individual to repent (or turn away from their sinful ways)? It would seem that if mere belief were the only requirement of heaven, then why would He not simply leave it at that?

I am not stating that belief in Him is not the only requirement, but I believe that it carries with it true repentance and willing obedience. The vast majority of Americans say they "believe" in Him, yet we're the most wretched and materialistic of all nations.

To repent is to reject the world; to believe is to accept God's will over your own. Any man going in the opposite direction of God's will has not repented and is thereby not worthy of Him (Luke 9:62).

Those who are arguing against repentance (which I have heard some of you do) with the case that after the cross, there's no need for repentance only believing, I advise you to read 2 Peter 3:9, "The Lord is not slack concerning his promise, as some men count slackness; but is longsuffering to us-ward, not willing that any should perish, but that all should come to *repentance.*" Revelation 9:20,21 says, "And the rest of the men which were not killed by these plagues yet *repented* not of the works of their hands, that they should not worship devils, and idols of gold, and silver... Neither *repented* they of their murders, nor of their sorceries, nor of their fornication, nor of their thefts." It seems repentance is a crucial requirement of salvation. May the LORD rebuke him whom preaches another doctrine to you.

A truly repentant man will despise sin if he has been changed from the inside. A superficial repentance or a lackluster faith will always show through a man's willingness to sin. A child of the King will not be as the slaves.

In Luke 24:49, Jesus says, "And behold, I send the promise of my Father upon you: but tarry ye in the city of Jerusalem, until ye be endued with power from on high." The word "endued" there in its original Greek is *enduo* (en-doo'-o) meaning, "(in the sense of *sinking* into a garment); to *invest* with clothing (lit. or fig.)." An alternative word would be "array" or "clothe (with);" another alternative is stated as "have (put) on."

These are very telling of the all-encompassing power and presence of the Holy Spirit in one's spirit and body upon salvation. It seems impossible to me to think that a person can be so embraced by the Holy Spirit of God and still live like every other wretched man in this world. Any person with any logical sense about them would easily come to the conclusion that a man not living a holy lifestyle cannot possibly have the Holy Spirit of God living within them. A Christian will live holy for the greater part of his/her existence; flesh will not have dominion over a true child of God, for (1 John 4:4) "...greater is he that is in you, than he that is in the world."

One thing I have found out clearly is that once an individual only seeks the will of God, they begin to feel no other way; they want nothing else. Sin becomes a disturbing thing. It disturbs the relationship between child and Father. If you are saved, then you have a Savior. This Savior has saved you from both your sinful nature and God's wrath. If you are not showing that you have been saved from your worldly lusts, then you have not been saved from your sinful nature, nor His wrath. You therefore have no Savior at all and are not saved, and will thereby not be saved from God's wrath. It's simple as that.

I have seen so many people claim to still be Christians because they prayed the sinner's prayer when they were twelve years old, but now they live like the rest of the world and have done so for twenty-plus years. The Holy Scriptures speak often of striving in faith unto perfection (Luke 8:14). After only three years of walking in the faith, I can attest to the fact of perfection being within grasp of any and every individual who has truly been reborn. I mean by perfection that one will not wilfully sin (Hebrews 10:26). They may have the occasional lustful thought or dream, or minor things, but even these things will be despised and hated by the true Christian whom walks in *the* faith.

To better solidify the meaning of "perfection," allow me to quote the very same Scripture as the apostle Paul in 2 Corinthians 6:17,18 when he is warning the congregation against mixing with sinners, saying, "Wherefore, come out from among them, and be ye separate, saith the Lord, and touch not the unclean thing; and I will receive you, and will be a Father unto you, and ye shall be my sons and daughters, saith the Lord Almighty."

Yet more clarification to what I have been stating throughout this book, none-the-less, it is 2 Corinthians 7:1 which I wish to emphasize, "Having therefore these promises, dearly beloved, let us cleanse ourselves from all filthiness of the flesh and spirit, perfecting holiness in the fear of God." Perfection and holiness are the same things. How do we attain both? The fear of the Lord. How do we attain the fear of the Lord? Abide in faith. It's quite plain when one reads the God's Word.

What are we saved by? Grace. Through what? Faith. (Ephesians 2:8). So it is by faith in the Son of God, Jesus Christ, whose faith justifies us before God. Every believer of the popularized O.S.A.S. quotes verse 9, "Not of works, lest any man should boast." But they never continue on to verse 10, "For we are his workmanship, created in Christ Jesus unto good works, which God hath before ordained that we should walk in them." It will show by the fruit in which the believer bears for the sake of our Lord Christ Jesus (go back to the *Faith* chapter to see biblical proof for this) as to whether the individual is in God's grace or not.

My argument is this: What happens when a person loses their faith? It is a necessity that one must have faith (which will show through the believer's life in doing God's will; they will bear good fruit, Matthew 7:20) in order to remain in God's grace. If faith is gone (as will be evidenced by the former believer doing their own will over God's will; *backsliding* would be a better word), then grace must also be gone.

The Israelites were saved from bondage out of Egypt; they then began their walk of faith towards the Promised Land. This is a type of a sinner being set free from the bondage of sin, then walking in faith until they finally reach the gates of heaven. But some of the Israelites lost faith in God along the way and were killed for turning back on God's will (Exodus 32).

I believe this signifies what happens to all whom cease in His will after God Himself has set the individual free from sin's grasp. Notice the penalty for the Israelites whom worshipped the god of gold (which is what most Christians worship to this day) and were killed by the Levites; God told Moses that their names are now blotted out of the book of life. My point in saying this is that the same happens to all whom turn their backs on God after He has so graciously set them free from bondage. For they were free to serve God, not free to do what they wanted.

In Matthew 12:37 it is written, "For by thy words thou shalt be justified, and by thy words thou shalt be condemned." Jesus tells the Pharisees in Matthew 12, it is a good tree that will bring forth good fruit; the tree is the person, their fruit, in this case, is their words. Once again, a telling thing of one showing through good works that they are with Christ, not merely relying on a night of prayer said years before, but upon one's willingness to do God's will. It seems such faith is place more in the prayer itself than in Christ, Whom they are praying to.

Paul speaks of justification being wrought of faith and not of works in Romans 4 and 5. I believe what he writes to be absolutely true, it is by faith that we are justified and within God's grace, but James touches up on the importance of faith being a thing in which can die after a certain point in a believer's life if left for the world.

When Paul states in Romans 5:9 that we are justified by the blood of Jesus, James' epistle only follows up on this point by stating in James 2:26, "For as the body without the spirit is dead, so faith without works is dead also." James does not add anything to, nor take away from what Paul states, but illustrates how faith is a living thing that can grow unto perfection. But just as it can be alive, it can also die, and once it is dead it is no more with a person, in which case, the person is found faithless, unjustified, and without God's grace.

Remember that faith is a thing in which is two parts combined - *intellectual* and *inward*. Most only have the intellectual, but not the inward. This is believing with the mind, but not with the heart (the Holy Spirit); therefore, as a result, they have not the outward, which is where the "good fruit" comes into play.

One quick note on justification is in James (2:21-25): He states that Abraham was justified after offering Isaac up for a sacrifice upon the altar; Rahab was justified after she had received the messengers and sent them out another way. What I would like to emphasize are the acts of these two themselves were a *showing* of their faith. One act happened after many years of serving God - for Abraham; the other was an act that happened rather abruptly and took not so much time - for Rahab. Still, the two were justified as their faith was shown through the fruit in which they exhibited. One need only to read James 2:18 to validate this claim, "...Thou hast faith, and I have works: shew me thy faith without thy works, and I will shew thee my faith by my works."

Because they had the *true* intellectual and inward faith, their members worked (on the outside) in accordance with what was on the inside. Their flesh did what God willed instead of what the world would have had them to do because *the* faith was truly present within them. They were justified by the faith, their works were a showing of their faith being true and sincere. The faith is the root; the works are the fruit. If the fruit no longer is growing, then it no longer has a connection to the root (which is Christ Jesus).

I also believe that James is illustrating the importance of obedience as well. If one has the faith, they will be obedient, but if they begin to be disobedient (backslide), then they will begin to lose the faith of the Son of God. They may even fully continue in their own intellectual belief *in* Christ, yet still be lacking and found wanting in relation to the faith *of* Christ.

A man can truly be reborn and be endued with the Holy Ghost in an instant after calling out to God. But, I believe that if they backslide and become disobedient to His will, this is when Satan's greatest trick comes into play. They maintain the *intellectual* part of faith (which is believing *in* Jesus Christ) but have lost the *inward* part of faith (which is the Holy Ghost conviction; belief *of* Jesus Christ) which is required for justification.

Satan's trick is enacted by reassuring the individual time after time of disobedient backsliding that they have both parts of the faith, when in reality they only have the intellectual part and not the all-important inward part.

This was the problem with me for 28 years of my "saved" life. I was doing the most ungodly acts a man can imagine, yet I still maintained that I was a heaven-bound Christian. I started out as a young teen on-fire for God, then fell into the world (and away from God) and continued to fall deeper because I had been told that nothing could take me out of the Father's hand, not even myself, therefore, I had no concern of God's will for my life.

Starting out, I openly proclaimed that Jesus was the Son of God and truly believed that He was God's Son and died for me, but after a time, I came to lose my faith and wound up not even knowing for sure if He ever existed at all. I lost my faith and, inevitably, fell from God's grace.

Paul was the greatest teacher on grace and the kindness of God outside of Jesus Christ, he wrote in Romans 6:1,2, "What shall we say then? Shall we continue in sin, that grace may abound? God forbid. How shall we, that are dead to sin, live any longer therein?" He then goes on in verses 15 and 16, "What then? shall we sin, because we are not under the law, but under grace? God forbid. Know ye not, that to whom ye yield yourselves servants to obey, his servants ye are to whom ye obey; whether of sin unto death, or of obedience unto righteousness?"

Towards the end of the chapter in verses 20 and 21, Paul states, "For when ye were the servants of sin, ye were free from righteousness. What fruit had ye then in those things whereof ye are now ashamed? for the end of those things is death."

Paul was not a superstar, but a Christian. He was a simple child of God. He never boasted of anything in which he himself could or would do. He never claimed to be a king, but a servant. In Galatians 1:10, he calls himself a *servant of Christ*. Being a servant meant that he did as Christ commanded him, not what he wanted to do. Because he did the works of his Master, everyone can tell of Whom he served - the LORD. He did not willingly sin and give in to his lusts. If his heart had turned to such things, this would have been an indication of his servitude to self and not to God.

If you serve sin you will sin willingly, even trying to justify the deeds of sinful servitude in any way possible in order to further continue in sin. If you serve

God, you will not wilfully sin; this is not to say that you will not sin again, but when you do, conviction will be present urging you away from doing that which gives you pleasure towards doing that which gives God pleasure, which is His righteous will and holiness.

When the Apostle advises Timothy on bishops and their characteristics, he states of how they should be sober and vigilant in 1 Timothy 3, but then in verse 6, he states the consequences of not being as such when he says, "Not a novice, lest being lifted up with pride he fall into the condemnation of the devil." But the condemnation of the devil is reserved for the unsaved, isn't it? Why then would Paul state such a thing? The only answer would be that it is possible to fall from God's grace and be condemned even after becoming a holy deacon in the Church of Christ. In the next verse he mentions the possibility of falling into the snare of the devil. These things are possible.

Luke 16:10-13, Christ states clearly, "He that is faithful in that which is least is faithful also in much: and he that is unjust in the least is unjust also in much. If therefore ye have not been faithful in the unrighteous mammon, who will commit to your trust the true riches?" These words alone are very telling. Jesus is stating that if you cannot be trusted with little, why should He trust you with much. If you cannot remain in God's will for a short time on earth, how can you be expected to do so in eternity? If you are not faithful in tithing out of a hundred dollars, why should the Ancient of Days trust you with an everlasting treasure?

He goes on, "And if ye have not been faithful in that which is another man's, who shall give you that which is your own? No servant can serve two masters: for either he will hate the one, and love the other; or else he will hold to one, and despise the other. Ye cannot serve God and mammon."

Galatians 3:10,11 tells us that all whom are under the law are cursed (emphasizing that no man can work to gain God's grace, only faith). Verse 12 tells us that Christ became that curse upon the cross for us (He took the burden of the law upon Himself and fulfilled it totally, ultimately becoming the only Door into God's eternal kingdom for all who go through Him in order to enter in).

Skip forward to Galatians 5 now: The opening verse exhorts us to *stand fast* in liberty, which is only found in Jesus Christ, not becoming a slave to sin by sinning. Verse 13 tells those living in Christ's liberty (walking in the Spirit) to not use such a gracious liberty for an occasion to sin. An indication of one walking in the Spirit and not in the flesh is described in Galatians 5:17.

Verse 18 is the verse in which I would like to emphasize in order to prove my point: "But if ye be led of the Spirit, ye are not under the law." Being led of the Spirit is carrying your cross and having faith in Christ; it is bearing good fruit in His name. But those whom are not carrying their cross are therefore deemed to be under the law.

To clarify my point, those whom have faith in Jesus Christ will walk in the Spirit - live righteous, holy, just, and saintly. If one's heart turns from this path to their own, then because the Spirit will not always strive with men, they are under the law (in the flesh) and not under God's grace. They are not part of the Body of Christ. This goes for the unrepentant sinners, and backsliders alike.

When we backslide, over time we become the *servant* of sin again, and not of God. If your faith rests in your job, family, friends, children, anything but God, then you should not believe that you are under His grace as your faith is not in Him (which is required of His grace).

So what are we saved from, and when? These are the two main points in which this entire writing has focused around. The answers to these questions: The bondage of this world – now; and God's wrath – upon death.

We are initially freed from our sinful lusts when we call out to God and believe in the name of His Son Jesus Christ (Acts 2:21). The Comforter (Holy Spirit) is sent by God into the new believer's life to cleanse them. Conviction begins to take place over pleasure of one's sins. This is part of the grace of God - to grant unto you the strength needed to overcome fleshly desires and, inevitably, the whole world, in the name of Jesus Christ. You then begin your walk of faith (2 Corinthians 5:7) and fruit bearing in Jesus' name. Obedience would be the key word for those whom walk by faith and the liberty in which is granted unto you is the liberty to no longer serve sin but God (1 Peter 2:16).

Matthew 7:21, Jesus says, "Not every one that saith unto me, Lord, Lord, shall enter into the kingdom of heaven; but he that doeth the will of my Father which is in heaven." Luke 6:46, Jesus says again, "And why call ye me, Lord, Lord, and do not the things which I say?" Jesus is implying here that only those whom do His will are to call Him *Lord*. Those of disobedience are not of His flock. After a life of reliance and faith in Jesus' name is lived, after the believer has fought the good fight, finished the course, and *kept* the faith (like Paul the apostle, 2 Timothy 4:7,8), then the crown of righteousness is laid up for all whom believe in Him.

A man can say anything. I, for instance, can say that I am a woman. Though I walk, talk, dress, speak, look, and act like a man, I can still claim that I am a woman. Though every bit of my being testifies to me being a man, I can still make such a claim, and completely believe the claim myself. But me making the claim does not change the fact that I am indeed a man. Nearly every individual I meet claims to be a Christian. Though they walk, talk, dress, speak, look, and act like an unrepentant sinner, they still claim to be a saint and child of the holy God. The same logic applies to them. If it looks like a duck, flies like a duck, swims like a duck, sounds like a duck, hangs out with and follows other ducks - it's a duck. Case closed.

Matthew 7:23 has been used on several occasions in an attempt to prove O.S.A.S., "And then will I profess unto them, I never knew you..." The emphasis is on the *never* aspect, in which they are implying that once Jesus knows an individual (and the individual knows Him) they are eternally secure. But Romans 1:21 states, "Because that, when they knew God, they glorified him not as God, neither were thankful; but became vain in their imaginations, and their foolish heart was darkened." Here we see that an individual can know God, or of God, yet still not be of His flock. This is a showing that even those whom know God, either spiritually and/or physically, can be found not glorifying Him, which is a reference to disobeying Him, thereby being rendered over to what Romans 1:26-32 states of being reprobate.

How can a person whom is calling out to Christ, and is at that moment crucified with Jesus (Galatians 2:20) and no longer living for themselves and completely allowing the Holy Spirit to do His work within them, any longer *dwell* in the sin of the world (1 John 3:9)? It's impossible. The Holy Spirit is holy, not of sin and the things of this world. The only conclusion a sensible person can come to is that the person's heart has turned from God, meaning they have turned from the ways of the Holy Spirit working within them, and, therefore, are not of God.

The "sinning saint" makes the grievous error of believing that holiness only lies ahead of life at the point when this sinful flesh is dead and we are glorified and made new. But it is not the flesh that sins. Ezekial 18:20 says, "The soul that sinneth, it shall die..." So it is the *soul* that sins (as you are your spirit/soul, and not your fleshly body); therefore, the body can only be blamed for the *temptations* in which the soul ultimately chooses to either ignore (for the LORD's sake) or act upon.

I also believe this verse to pertain to the death in which is mentioned so often in accordance to sin in the New Testament. The preachers of O.S.A.S. often say that it is the body in which experiences death if one backslides and falls away from God, not the soul. But Ezekial 18:20 begs to differ that statement. It is the *soul* that chooses sin over God's will which experiences death (the second death - hell). I believe Galatians 6:8 can also be a New Testament verse in which verifies this claim.

Many whom take the stance of the popularized O.S.A.S. doctrine use such verses John 10:28, "And I give unto them eternal life; and they shall never perish, neither shall any man pluck them out of my hand." But let us look at the verse preceding 28, John 10:27 states, "My sheep hear my voice, and I know them, and they follow me." Following Him points right back to fruit bearing in His name. How often does Christ emphasize denying this world, even denying ourselves, and following Him?

Jesus says in Luke 13:24, "Strive to enter in at the strait gate: for many, I say unto you, will seek to enter in, and shall not be able." This He spoke of is the gate of heaven and the difficulty mankind has in entering it. The word I would like to emphasize is *strive*; the original Greek word for this "strive" is *agonizomai* (ag-o-nid'-zom-ahee) meaning "to struggle," with an alternative English word being *fight*.

This indicates an ongoing and continuous struggle and battling towards the objective of reaching the strait gate (heaven). There is nothing lax in its meaning. But, the teaching of *once saved, always saved* these days leaves most of its believers with a mindset based upon callousness and lazy attitudes, in which they are more fixated upon God's grace over God's will. Once again, I would relate this back to the lack of fear in which they have of God; for this they are rather slothful in doing His will, but seem anxious in doing their own.

For those of you who have an urgency to do the Lord's will, I salute you; but to those of whom I speak of, I will relate to Proverbs 21:25, "The desire of the slothful killeth him; for his hands refuse to labor." If a man's demise transpires due to him refusing to do that which he must for himself, how much more of death will the man experience whom refuses to do that which he must for God? Faith is the root of such fervency in doing God's will and those whom bear not His fruit have not such a root, and, thereby, have not faith.

One final terrifying point in which I would like to emphasize is the *many* in which Jesus is speaking of. This is not to the atheists, agnostics, Satanists, evolutionists, Muslim or Hindu believers, New Agers, etc. This is to the professing Christians. Those whom are down here right now saying, "I love the Lord. I'm His child. I believe in Him. I'm saved. We're all sinners, but He's a forgiving God."

Many of you even call Him Father and may even go to church and tithe, but you do what you want to do and not what His will is for you to do. You are wasting your time. Be either cold or hot, but not lukewarm towards Him. I believe He will be more merciful to the greatest atheist in that day than the self-deceived Christian whom makes light of His commandments.

At least the atheist isn't a wolf in sheep's clothing. He's an obvious wolf and does not attempt to appear as a sheep, an obvious bad guy who is not an ignorant stumbling block leading others to perdition.

One of my favorite preachers (who believed in the popularized O.S.A.S.) once quoted verse 28 and stated, "I think it would be a strange type of eternal life if I had it today and didn't have it tomorrow." But our lives are only eternal after this temporary life has passed. I am trying to get across that it is after a believer has walked by faith in Jesus Christ, in the will of God, having endured and, through the Holy Spirit, overcome this world and all of the pleasures within it to do solely God's will, it is at that point that they will be saved from hell. It is at that point that no man shall pluck them out of the Hand that keeps them. Until then, self-examine yourself as to whether you are saved in the other sense – from the bondage of this world.

Are you saved from a sinful lifestyle and freely serving God? Are you saved from Satan's grip and freely resting in the shadow of the Father's wings? He whom the Son sets free is free indeed! This means in all ways, not free to sin and become disobedient. Your freedom is the freedom to do what you could not do before you attained such a great salvation – to have a good conscience toward God and serve Him – which you could not do before He gave you the Comforter to do so.

No man whom has ever lived has been able to try to be a Christian and succeed. It is a lifestyle not of *trying* to please God, but of *wanting* to please God. Your heart must be changed and only God can do the work. We need not seek any greater miracle than the great transformation of a rotten sinner seeking destruction into a God-fearing man walking in firm obedience all the days of his life; and it's all God's work. Man need only choose to abide in His glory.

I would now like to address a verse I have heard emphasized so many times by Eternal Security preachers, Ephesians 4:30 states, "And grieve not the holy Spirit of God, whereby ye are sealed unto the day of redemption." Whenever I have heard this verse quoted it is often misquoted or misunderstood as one being sealed "until" the day of redemption, not "unto." This is where the preachers err greatly. The original Greek there for "unto" is *eis* meaning "for" not "until" as so many I have heard preach.

The word "sealed" used here in its original writing is *sphragizo* (sfrag-id'-zo) meaning what is implied, "to stamp (with a signet or private mark)." It is a seal like on a letter and just like any seal can be broken or removed. Those who quote this verse out of context tend to overlook the entire fourth chapter of Ephesians that clearly shows a conditional state in which the believers (those sealed for the day of redemption) are to follow accordingly.

Circumcision was also a "seal" placed on the Jews in the Old Testament as a promise of redemption, but Romans 2:25 says, "For circumcision verily profiteth, if thou keep the law: but if thou be a breaker of the law, thy circumcision is made uncircumcision." meaning the seal counts for nothing if one becomes a transgressor and enemy of God. Seals can be broken is my point.

When "grieve" is spoken of towards the Holy Spirit, forget not that one can do so to the extent of insulting and becoming worse off than before they were ever sealed (see Hebrews 10:29). This is a form of blasphemy, as taking the LORD's name in vain is not merely done by speaking, but by our actions after we have taken the Holy name of God and call ourselves Christians and children of God, then turn to living like the world again.

In 2 Timothy 3:12, Paul attest to what Jesus Christ said, saying, "Yea, and all that will live godly in Christ Jesus shall suffer persecution." The Church is persecuted everywhere else in the world except America. I do not believe it to be due to America being so pious and earnest in doing God's will, quite the contrary, we are the most wicked of all nations. Nearly all of the Christians in America are fake and self-deceived. They attend church and live just like the world every moment outside of it. They watch the occasional Christian movie or televangelist on the idiot box and believe they have a mansion waiting for them.

In 2 Timothy 2:3-6, "Thou therefore endure hardness, as a good soldier of Jesus Christ. No man that warreth entangleth himself with the affairs of this life; that he may please him who hath chosen him to be a soldier. And if a man also strive for masteries, yet is he not crowned, except he strive lawfully. The husbandman that laboureth must be first partaker of the fruits." Simply put: Endure persecution on Christ's behalf; No man that serves Him will become like the worldly men; a man will not receive the prize unless he is faithful to Jesus Christ our Lord; only the hard-working farmer will partake of the crops. Abiding (enduring) in faith until the end is the gist of these verses.

Revelation 2, Jesus consistently speaks to the churches about overcoming (being faithful to Him) through trials and tribulations before the gift of eternal life is granted unto them:

Verse 7, "... To him that overcometh will I give to eat of the tree of life, which is in the midst of the paradise of God."

Verse 10, "... be thou faithful unto death, and I will give thee a crown of life."

Verse 11, "... He that overcometh shall not be hurt of the second death."

Verse 17, "... To him that overcometh will I give to eat of the hidden manna, and will give him a white stone, and in the stone a new name written, which no man knoweth saving he that receiveth it."

Verse 23, "...I will give unto everyone of you according to your works." Obedient or disobedient, He will give accordingly.

Verse 26, "And he that overcometh, and keepeth my works unto the end, to him will I give power over the nations: And he shall rule them with a rod of iron; as the vessels of a potter shall they be broken shivers: even as I received of my Father. And I will give him the morning star."

Revelation 3 continues: verse 5, "He that overcometh, the same shall be clothed in white raiment; and I will not blot out his name of the book of life, but I will confess his name before my Father, and before his angels."

Verse 11, "Behold, I come quickly: hold that fast which thou hast, that no man take thy crown."

Verse 12, "Him that overcometh will I make a pillar in the temple of my God, and he shall go no more out: and I will write upon him the name of my God, and the name of the city of my God, which is new Jerusalem, which cometh down out of heaven from my God: and I will write upon him my new name."

Verse 21, "To him that overcometh will I grant to sit with me in my throne, even as I also overcame, and am set down with my Father in his throne."

Paul speaks of salvation from God's wrath coming to the believer at the end of their life in Romans 6:22, "But now being made free from sin, and become servants to God, ye have your fruit unto holiness, and the end everlasting life."

Remember what I told you just a bit ago about what one of my favorite preachers said, "I think it would be a strange type of eternal life if I had it today and didn't have it tomorrow;" Well, Paul is clearly stating here that everlasting life comes at the *end* of life, not the moment that you are reborn. So it is upon death that the believer is *saved* from God's wrath. This comes after faithfully enduring and overcoming the temptations and persecutions of this world and showing yourself approved and chosen through Jesus Christ our Lord.

Also in Hebrews 3:14, "For we are made partakers of Christ, if we hold the beginning of our confidence stedfast unto the end;" Hebrews 6 says in verses 11-15, "And we desire that every one of you do shew the same diligence to the full assurance of hope unto the end: That ye be not slothful, but followers of them who through faith and patience inherit the promises. For when God made promise to Abraham, because he could swear by no greater, he sware by himself, saying, Surely blessing I will bless thee, and multiplying I will multiply thee. And so, after he had patiently endured, he obtained the promise." Once again, through steadfast patience in the faith one inherits the promises. Not momentarily believing in God then leaving His will.

Matthew 7:14, Christ says, "Because strait is the gate, and narrow is the way, which leadeth unto life, and few there be that find it." I have heard so many Eternal Security preachers speak on the strait gate, but they never mention the narrow way. This narrow way is our walk of faith until the end. It is possible to fall off or draw back from this narrow path, as it is a faithful reliance on Christ Jesus while carrying our own cross in His glorious name. It's found to be too difficult for most whom journey down it. But it is this narrow path (faithful walk) that must be taken for an individual to reach eternal life.

People believe salvation to be giving Jesus all your sins. But it is not that, no, not at all. Jesus won the victory over sin and death two thousand years ago on the cross. You give Him you; your every thought, love, desire, your very being becomes His and is no longer yours. He saves you from you. Because He knows what is best for you, you don't. Ultimately, He saves you from yourself for Himself. He has already won the victory for all. Our part is to accept His sacrifice. Our prize is Him and all things; His prize is us.

I would like to close this chapter with clarification on what I believe. I do believe in Eternal Security, the difference between my belief and the popular belief is that I do not believe it to be unconditional. I do not believe that the grace of God gives His children a license to sin. Where true faith is present, so is obedience. Where faith is found to be dead due to prolonged disobedience leading to a change of heart from God's will to the lusts and love of the world, then I believe one can, and will, fall from grace and therefore have no salvation awaiting them. This is where we differ.

CHAPTER 12

CONCLUSION

To the One whom I love and adore, and He loves me ever more. I shall endeavor to do Thy will O King! It is You, and Thou alone, that I place all of my confidence! For I am but dust and ashes before Thee! The Lamb is my love and King unto which I sing and dance. Blessed art Thou above heaven and the earth, forever and ever! Amen

You have heard it said that God is going to restore the world after the Great White Throne Judgment to how He initially began it before the fall of man with the New Heaven and New Earth – this I do believe to a great extent and will not argue against. Thus, I would proclaim that God now seeks the hearts in which would *not* partake of the tree of knowledge of good and evil. In other words, those whom choose obedience to Him over their own ways, thoughts, and imaginations. Those whom choose the tree of life over the other.

My ultimate cry - repent! Those whom live like the world will die with the world. You bear bad fruit - you are a bad branch and must be burned. Be not deceived: there is a teaching pervading the earth and has become popular for a reason. All over the radio they stress that the popular O.S.A.S. belief is the true way to heaven, but where is the revival? Where is the holiness? Where is the light? Where are the prayers? Where is the fear of God? It almost doesn't exist anymore due to this belief that one can still go to heaven no matter what they do after they pray the sinner's prayer; even if they become faithless!

It is no coincidence that the "prosperity" preachers, "purpose-driven" and "emergent" mega-churches all preach the popularized O.S.A.S. belief. This being Satan's world, it is no surprise that he would reward those who teach his greatest trick to the masses. It's the easiest and most convenient way that I can think of to get into heaven. It's as if you can say the sinner's prayer then check it off the list of things to do in life. It's a temporal matter of faith applied to a lifelong requirement of abiding within that same faith (1 Corinthians 4:2).

The majority of Baptists also believe this, I know, because I have grown up in a Baptist family and was taught it my entire life. There are many people that I know who hold to this belief and are still very devout Christians. They faithfully do God's will every day and hate it when they do not. Theirs is the kingdom of heaven. I am not saying that everyone who believes the popularized O.S.A.S. is hell-bound. I am only stressing the necessity of God's will above all things. God's will cannot be done without faith and we are saved by God's grace through the faith of His Son Jesus Christ.

I cannot stress enough that I am not teaching works to gain salvation, but let us remember that those who bear bad fruit are not worthy to be branches of Christ Jesus - The true Vine. For Jesus said in John 14:10, "Believest thou not that I am in the Father and the Father in me? the words that I speak unto you I speak not of myself: but the Father that dwelleth in me, he doeth the works."

Though they witnessed Jesus doing the works, He said it is the Father's works, and not His own. The same goes for the saints of God; it is not our works, but His works through us. Once we cease in doing His work on this earth, it must be that either our bodies are dead or the faith that was within us is dead. The latter being far more disastrous to the soul than the former could ever be!

Like 1 Corinthians 6:9,10, Paul states in 2 Timothy 3 many who are obviously (based on their character) not part of those destined for heaven. He says, "This know also, that in the last days perilous times shall come. For men shall be lovers of their own selves, covetous, boasters, proud, blasphemers, disobedient to parents, unthankful, unholy, without natural affection, truce-breakers, false accusers, incontinent, fierce, despisers of those that are good, traitors, heady, highminded, lovers of pleasures more than lovers of God; Having a form of godliness, but denying the power thereof: from such turn away."

He judged all of these by their works and deemed them not part of the family of God. Many do I know which claim the title Christian ("having a form of godliness") and fit into many of these characteristics ("but denying the power thereof"). From such - turn away.

In Romans 2:6-10, Paul speaks of God's judgment on both the faithful and unrepentant, "Who will render to every man according to his deeds: To them who by patient continuance in well doing seek for glory and honour and immortality, eternal life: But unto them that are contentious, and do not obey the truth, but obey unrighteousness, indignation and wrath, tribulation and anguish, upon every soul of man that doeth evil, of the Jew first, and also of the Gentile. But glory, honour, and peace, to every man that worketh good, to the Jew first, and also to the Gentile:"

Throughout the Holy Bible there are clear distinctions made between the characteristics of the children of God and everyone else. You can easily distinguish the two groups by the fruit they bear.

Know that I do this for all your sakes, beloved. I gain no glory from this, no honor from man; no women will adore me for telling you to walk in faith all the days of your life in humble obedience to Christ and Him only. Of such things, the world may hate me - that's fine. My family may even view me in a different manner, but of such, I am unmoved. I shall face the Lord with a smile on that day. All that matters now is Him - nothing else. I would encourage you to feel the same and follow Jesus Christ.

I would like to repeat that which I have already stated: I do not believe that our works are what count, but belief in Jesus Christ that works repentance. It is His works, not ours that are done in His name after the Comforter comes into the believer's life. All glory, power, and honor go to Him and not us once we begin to believe. Before the Comforter comes into a person's life, all of your deeds and works are for you and are your temporal rewards.

Remember what Jesus said of the prayers the Pharisee's would pray publicly. They would be highly esteemed and admired by the people. Jesus speaks of this by stating (Matthew 6:5), "Verily I say unto you, They have their reward." Before I repented, I was the most foul-mouthed, fornicating drug addict, completely self-absorbed and apathetic to all people; I even believed in evolution and was slowly becoming an agnostic; I was the worst of the worst; then I called out to God again - now I'm a preacher! Glory, glory!!! Hallelujah! Only Christ's Spirit could do such a thing! I now do what I then despised, because God is working through me. I'm living because I'm dying - how lovely!

There's nothing that we can do in order for the Holy Spirit to come into our lives other than truly believe in Jesus Christ as Lord and Savior. After that, the Holy Spirit is called the Comforter, signifying that He helps us to be faithful and, thereby, righteous among the wicked in order for us to do Christ's work on His behalf. All works that we do while in the flesh (before being reborn and faithful) are counted as nothing in light of eternity.

After rebirth, it is only Christ's work being done, and this can only be done in the faithful (those whom choose God's will over everything). The faithful are those that have grace from God and do His will. Faith brings the fear of the Lord, trust in the Lord, discernment between what is of God and what is of evil, the desire to do His will and be obedient, it keeps conviction, it makes one righteous through Jesus Christ, and, ultimately, the great reward of eternal life.

We are not to hold on to any sin after the rebirth into the Body of the Lord Jesus Christ. In Matthew 13:44, Jesus tells us a parable, "Again, the kingdom of heaven is like unto treasure hid in a field; the which when a man hath found, he hideth, and for joy thereof goeth and selleth all that he hath, and buyeth that field." So a person is to give away all that they covet - mentally, spiritually, emotionally, physically, etc. - and in return, receive all of Jesus; His will and His promises (which is where faith comes in) become more apparent. The less of us we have, the more of Him we receive.

Lukewarm Christians today are unwilling to give anything away for Christ. They are comfortable and perfectly fit the description of the Laodicean Church in Revelation 3. The popularized O.S.A.S. followers are taught that they need not do anything more than say the sinner's prayer and, no matter what they do after that, they'll be in heaven, leaving them utterly shocked afterwards as to why they are in hell forever.

When Christ encounters the rich young ruler (Matthew 19:16-22), He tells him to give all that he has away and follow Him. The young rich man walked away full of sorrow because he had great wealth. Today's Church is filled with young rich rulers such as this: They wish not to step outside of their comfort zones, spread the gospel, suffer persecution like Jesus

Christ said, yet they wish to obtain the everlasting reward of eternal life afterwards still.

I write this book because I believe that we have placed so much emphasis on grace that we have forgotten about faith or, at least, its true meaning. We have lost the fear of God because we now depend upon what preachers tell us instead of what God says.

Upon my initial completion of this book, I told several folks about what I now gather from Scriptures in accordance to salvation. All of them, or at least, 9 out of 10 of them believed in the popularized version of O.S.A.S.. Since me quoting for them verse after verse of the Word of God clarifying what true salvation is, they have completely become on-fire for Christ. I now see them fearing the Lord and being better Christians than I have ever seen them. They get up and go to church now, when before they didn't pay it much more attention than to simply feel a little down because they didn't get up and go again; they tithe; they aren't cursing; etc.

It is that fear of the Lord that is the beginning of wisdom, and without knowledge people perish (Hosea 4:6). I praised God when I began to see the fruits of this teaching! O, what a glory to do God's will and see it become fruitful within one person, but I have since seen dozens of people place God first and foremost in their lives again. No words can express the joy! Such ineffable glory cannot be found in this physical realm without God's help! Hallelujah!!!

Now let's go on: Many are taught that faith is simply believing that Jesus is real, the Son of God, was crucified, buried, and resurrected. They seem to overlook the fact that faith is the foundation for the servant to do God's will - "faith without works is dead." If your faith does not carry with it the willingness to do God's will then it is either not *the* faith, or is weak and will inevitably turn to the person's will. This is disobedience and of Satan, not God.

It is more than simply sitting around and believing in God and acknowledging that Jesus Christ is His Son and that the Bible is truly the Word of God. If simply believing intellectually were the only requirement, then even fallen angels would be allowed entry into heaven (James 2:19). They are *not* due to them falling away from God. Any reader of Hebrews 6 would become frightened with the knowledge of verses 4-6:

"For it is impossible for those who were once enlightened, and have tasted of the heavenly gift, and were made partakers of the Holy Ghost, and have tasted the good word of God, and the powers of the world to come, if they shall fall away, to renew them again unto repentance; seeing they crucify to themselves the Son of God afresh, and put him to an open shame."

Many whom believe the same teachings as I (to an extent) have quoted these verses, but go further, my brothers: Verses 7 and 8 say, "For the earth which drinketh in the rain that cometh oft upon it, and bringeth forth herbs meet for them by whom it is dressed, receiveth blessing from God: But that which beareth thorns and briers is rejected, and is nigh unto cursing; whose end is to be burned." The rain is like the Holy Spirit pouring blessing upon the men. The herbs is the works of God being manifested in men; the thorns and briers is disobedience, even though the same Spirit poured down upon them as well. The herbs are blessed; the thorns and briers are burned. A chilling illustration!

I was asked if I believe that verses 5 & 6 are teaching that it is *impossible* for them to who have been reborn, once they *fall away*, for them to be *renewed* (reborn) and come back into the fold. I would relate to what Jesus says in Luke 11, "When the unclean spirit is gone out of a man, he walketh through dry places, seeking rest; and finding none, he saith, I will return unto my house whence I came out. And when he cometh, findeth it swept and garnished. Then goeth he, and taketh to him seven other spirits more wicked than himself; and they enter in, and dwell there: and the last state of that man is worse than the first."

How many supposed Christians have we all seen whom are now worse off than they were before they were saved? They were so on-fire for God, now they are the greatest of all sinners. Try speaking to them now; they are completely fallen from God, not the same as before. I believe once a man loses the conviction of the Holy Ghost, and falls completely away from God and into the world, it is at that point that so many spirits have inhabited him that it is then 'impossible' for him to be renewed by the Spirit of God. I believe this to be a form of blasphemy of the Holy Ghost and unforgivable in the eyes of God. Notice how Jesus finishes this message by saying (verse 28) "...blessed are they that hear the word of God, and keep it."

There is also the matter of the reprobate mind in which God renders such over to. Like Paul describes in Romans 1:28, there are many instances in which God renders people over to their sins because their hearts are so hardened to the Holy Ghost. I mention this to bring attention to the dangers of backsliding, which is where many will believe a lie (such as I am exposing in this book) and be damned.

When Paul mentions in 1 Thessalonians 5:19, "Quench not the Spirit." let us recall what the original Greek word implies there by "quench." The original word is *sbennumi* (sben'-noo-mee) meaning, "to extinguish" with an alternate English translation of "go out." The same original word is used also by Paul in Ephesians 6:16 when he refers to extinguishing the fiery darts of the wicked with the shield of faith. He does not simply imply with that word a mere toning down of the fiery darts; he means a complete "putting out" of them. The same meaning is used in relation to the Holy Spirit in his letter to the Thessalonians. My point being, once again, that it is possible for a man to insult the Holy Spirit to the point of "extinguishing" Him altogether.

Jesus says in John 15:16, "Ye have not chosen me, but I have chosen you, and ordained you, that ye should go and bring forth fruit, and that your fruit should remain..." We do not get to go to heaven because we pray a prayer one night at the altar in church. We first must be called (Holy Spirit convicted), then we are given the opportunity to choose to take up our own cross and deny ourselves and the things of this world (calling out to God for salvation; repenting), then abiding in the faith until the end - then we are glorified in heaven. This is sanctification, justification, and glorification in a nutshell.

Jesus chooses us because we have been found faithful to Him, and in Him, obedient, obeyed the Father and done the Father's will. Being omniscient, He of course knew whom He would elect before the foundation of the world, so think not that I'm implying a period of waiting on us from God.

Heaven will be beautiful and beyond imagination, Paul states in 1 Corinthians 2:9, "...Eye hath not seen, nor ear heard, neither have entered into the heart of man, the things which God hath prepared for them that love him." Notice it is written, "for them that *love* him;" now let us recall what Jesus said in John 14:15, "If ye love me, keep my commandments." Here we see a relation between loving God and keeping His commandments. One can only question whether such love, and ultimately, salvation itself, is present within an individual if they do not keep the commandments of God (walk in the Spirit).

James 1:12 is further evidence of salvation pertaining only to those who love God (by word and action, not only by word). He says in it, "Blessed is the man that endureth temptation: for when he is tried, he shall receive the crown of life, which the Lord hath promised to them that love him." Notice also it mentions enduring temptation in relation to receiving the crown of life.

Romans 8:1 is often quoted by teachers of the popularized Eternal Security belief, it says, "There is therefore now no condemnation to them which are in Christ Jesus, who walk not after the flesh, but after the Spirit." They seem to only read the first half of the verse, but the second half, "who walk not after the flesh, but after the Spirit" is the most significant to those whom have read Paul's chapter 6 of Romans. So the first half only pertains to those who walk in the

Spirit. If you so freely walk in the flesh, then let that be a showing of where your heart is.

Who is more unlike God than Satan? What was Satan's problem - he wanted to stop listening to the Father and do his own thing. Why then can we think that we can be like the devil - turn from doing God's will - and believe that we still will be allowed into heaven?

Satan was called Lucifer - one of the most glorious angels ever created by the LORD God. Lucifer probably did the most powerful and beautiful things for God. But when iniquity was found in this glorified being's heart he was cast away from the Father. This iniquity was the yearning to do what he wanted and not what God willed. He was not seeking entrance into heaven (as we are), but was already in heaven, fully enjoying the fruits of the Father. Still, he was cast out...

To further solidify the fact of their being certain character traits in which one can see who is and isn't saved, let us look at Revelation 21:7,8, "He that overcometh shall inherit all things; and I will be his God, and he shall be my son. But the fearful, and unbelieving, and the abominable, and murderers, and whoremongers, and sorcerers, and idolaters, and all liars, shall have their part in the lake which burneth with fire and brimstone: which is the second death."

The reason for me being so dogmatic in pointing out these certain character traits is to show that continuously bearing such wicked fruit, be it of an outright sinner or a once-blessed Christian, these are the characteristics of those whom have not the Holy Spirit within their hearts. How can a man claim to have the everlasting Father living within him and be a sorcerer, or drunkard, or liar? Of such - turn away!

It is very possible for one to fall away from God even after being so close to Him. I have witnessed so many go up to the altar broken, be on-fire for God and filled with the Spirit, only to turn right back to their old ways after a couple of years - like a dog to his vomit; like a sow to the mud.

2 Peter 2:20-22 says, "For if after they have escaped the pollutions of the world through the knowledge of the Lord and Savior Jesus Christ, they are again entangled therein, and overcome, the latter end is worse with them than the beginning. For it had been better for them not to have known the way of righteousness, than, after they have known it, to turn from the holy commandment delivered unto them. But it is happened unto them according to the true proverb, The dog is turned to his own vomit again; and the sow that was washed to her wallowing in the mire."

There are those who argue that God will not blot any names out of the book of life - I disagree. This is stated in both the Old and New Testament. God told

Moses in Exodus 32:33 that He would blot the names out of those who sinned against Him from His book. In Revelation 3:5, Jesus says that He will not blot out his name that overcomes from His book. Also, Revelation 22:19 says, "And if any man shall take away from the words of the book of this prophecy, God shall take away his part out of the book of life, and out of the holy city..." the "holy city" is the New Jerusalem (Heaven); This testifies to the warning also being for the children of God, not only for the unbelieving.

I have heard from some how the Lamb's book of life and the book of life mentioned in these two cases are different (please read Revelation 17:8 for clarification of this *book of life* being the same as the *Lamb's book of life*), even so, these verses imply that He could blot them out of any book if He so wished (like He said, we have not chosen Him, He has chosen us, meaning that it is by His good grace that we are written in the book). Though it is known to God, it is upon us to be sober and vigilant, through fear and trembling, to abide in the faith of Christ until He confesses our name to the Father.

Galatians 6:7,8 says, "Be not deceived; God is not mocked: for whatsoever a man soweth, that shall he also reap. For he that soweth to his flesh shall of the flesh reap corruption; but he that soweth to the Spirit shall of the Spirit reap life everlasting." A clear telling of those things in which we sow in this life being reaped not only in this life but in the next, for that is where our hearts lied.

If by this point all of the evidence in which I have shown unto you has not convinced you of the manner of true salvation through Jesus Christ our Lord, then I can only conclude that your decision is made and mind cannot see God's Word over your preacher's words. I still request a bit more of your time...

Love God. Grow in grace through prayer, assembling, studying the Bible, giving, and forgiving; by doing these things you will show yourself approved of God. Like David requested to be purged with hyssop, sin must be scrubbed out and uprooted entirely if repentance is to have any effect. Flood your mind and soul with holy music and praise God for everything! This will assure you are blameless at all times so that the Father God and His Son Jesus Christ will be pleased with you if you were to be before Him in a moment's notice. Do His will and not yours, for if you begin to do your own will – woe unto you. I must repeat – repent! – and turn from that which is keeping you from Him. This is the blessed assurance and only way to know you are eternally secure due to the peace which passes all understanding residing in your heart.

One of the last messages given to us from the Word of God is said in Revelation 22:14, "Blessed are they that do his commandments, that they may have right to the tree of life, and may enter in through the gates into the city."

A few things in this verse need to be pointed out: First, the obvious - the emphasis in which is given towards doing His commandments (not simply saying a little prayer, this I have been stating the entire book); Second, notice that it says "commandments" with an "s," I point this out to show that he is speaking of *all* the commandments of God and not simply the one in which many quote (1 John 3:23) out of context. Check the verses before and after that verse before quoting it and you will see the truth of it's context.

So the tree of life is withheld from those who do not faithfully believe and keep His commandments? I believe so. This goes back to the bearing of fruit, glorifying God, denying self, taking up your cross, and so forth, once again, no emphasis on anything on our behalf except us choosing Him over everything else. For the greatest of commandments is what Jesus said in Matthew 22:37, "Thou shalt love the Lord thy God with all thy heart, and with all thy soul, and with all thy mind."

2 Peter 1:9,10 says, "But he that lacketh [faith, virtue, knowledge, temperance, patience, godliness, kindness, charity] is blind, and cannot see afar off, and hath forgotten that he was purged from his old sins. Wherefore the rather, brethren, give diligence to make

your calling and election *sure*: for if ye do these things, ye shall never fall." This is what I have been attempting to be as thorough about in accordance to true salvation as possible: Make certain through doing God's will that you are saved. Leave not such an important thing as your soul at risk of destruction, beloved!

I have said this before and I'll say it 'til my temple is dead on this earth: Faith will bring forth the fear of the Lord. Those whom use foul language continually and proclaim to be Christian; those whom cannot wait to leave church to defile their bodies; those whom use drugs and drink alcohol and still proclaim the Christian life have little to no fear of the Lord. I righteously judge them now as being at the very least weak in the faith, and in grave danger! They claim to have faith, yet have no fear of God; therefore, they have little strength in faith and risk falling from grace. Calling yourself a Christian does not make you a Christian! Now let us conclude this.

2 Thessalonians 2:3 says of the last days, "Let no man deceive you by any means: for that day shall not come, except there come a falling away first..." He spoke this of the day of the Lord implying the last days of the age of man. The *falling away* is, in my opinion, what is transpiring now among the churches. I believe this will increase drastically in the coming days for various reasons, one of which relating to the masses believing in a pre-tribulation rapture, which

I do not think can be found out-rightly in the Holy Bible. But that is another case for another time.

Have you not noticed that we are the weakest Church age ever? Any in doubt of the vast majority of "Christians" being self-deceived need only to look at the statistics of divorce rate: we are identical to the world. I do not believe this to be due to everybody backsliding. I do not believe this to be due to everybody being lukewarm. I believe they are no longer, or have never been, true Christians at all. I even know of "Christians" having abortions. Go to the jailhouse - every inmate and crooked cop's a Christian. Ask a room full of strippers and drug addicts, I bet half of them claim they're Christians.

I cannot stress my sadness at seeing the conformity of the Church to the worldly ways. Though Jesus speaks of the trials and tribulation of the Church in Matthew 10:22, what He says is very telling in that He places great emphasis on abiding until the end, just as He speaks in the Vine parable of John 15, when He says, "And ye shall be hated of all men for my name's sake: but he that endureth to the end shall be saved."

The popularized doctrine of *once saved, always saved* is the greatest, and most potent, of all tricks in which Satan could have conjured up to deceive the potential and true Christians, in my opinion. My brethren, we are in the midst of the great falling away. We are the Laodicean Church!

In Revelation 3:15-21, Christ is speaking to the Laodicean church - the last church - us. This church is labeled as *lukewarm*, which is both hot and cold, implying a half-Christian, half-worldly person. There will be no part-time Christians allowed into heaven. This is the Church of our day and one of the primary reasons I believe this book is being inspired as of right now.

The Lord says, "I know thy works, that thou art neither cold nor hot: I would thou wert cold or hot. So then because thou art lukewarm, and neither cold nor hot, I will spue thee out of my mouth. Because thou sayest, I am rich, and increased with goods, and have need of nothing; and knowest not that thou art wretched, and miserable, and poor, and blind, and naked: I counsel thee to buy of me gold tried in the fire, that thou mayest be rich; and white raiment, that thou mayest be clothed, and that the shame of thy nakedness do not appear; and annoint thine eyes with eyesalve, that thou mayest see. As many as I love, I rebuke and chasten: be zealous therefore, and repent. Behold, I stand at the door, and knock: if any man hear my voice, and open the door, I will come in to him, and will sup with him, and he with me. To him that overcometh will I grant to sit with me in my throne, even as I also overcame, and am set down with my Father in his throne."

We now live in the most lazy and repugnant Church age in history. At no other time have we been so distracted and dead. Even the best preachers are deceived by a doctrine in which could be sending more people to hell than any other on earth. These verses are the perfect description of our time. We have more money, but less faith; we have more technology, but less passion; we have more science, but less God.

I would emphasize the most obvious of these verses, that is, the lukewarm being vomited out of His mouth. I believe this to be so significant to the concept I have been attempting to convey to the reader. Notice first how Jesus says from where He would vomit the lukewarm out of - His mouth - meaning they are already within His Body (they are of the children of God). Christ will show more mercy to the outright "cold" sinner on the day of Judgment over the "lukewarm" Christian.

Lukewarm is the condition of the Body of Christ today - they have conformed to the worldly lusts and desires and have lost the will to do His will. It is these who He rejects and spews out of His Body - the conformed Christian. Those in whom claim the title and once knew the Holy Ghost but left Him for the world. I believe this perfectly illustrates the reality that a truly reborn child of God can fall from His grace.

The difference between what I believe of the Eternal Security doctrine and the popularized version of it is this: If the world at large remains believing that a faithful prayer can be said and, after that, nothing you can do in this life (even losing that same faith) can take you away from Jesus Christ, then we will remain stagnant, confused, lukewarm, and in extreme danger afterwards of God's eternal wrath. But if the Church takes the Holy Bible for what it says and ceases in taking verses out of context to suit themselves - revival can begin, holiness comes back, we begin to faithfully pray and fear the Lord once more with all sobriety and diligence being truly led by, while abiding in, the Holy Spirit - That is true eternal security.

God of peace be with you all, amen!

About the Author

Stephen Pippin is a young minister and author who was born and raised in the countryside of Cookeville, Tennessee. He is a former lyricist and artist who struggled with years of trials and tribulations, even to the extent of becoming an outright agnostic and evolutionist. By God's good grace, Stephen was miraculously saved from such beliefs. He now spreads the good news to all who will hear.